GERALD DWORKIN

Massachusetts Institute of Technology

DETERMINISM, FREE WILL, AND MORAL RESPONSIBILITY

1970

Prentice-Hall, Inc., Englewood Cliffs, New Jersey

Library of Congress Catalog Card Number: 71-113848

Printed in the United States of America

C 13-202838-7
P 13-202820-4

Current Printing (last digit):
10 9 8 7 6 5 4 3 2 1

PRENTICE-HALL INTERNATIONAL, INC., London
PRENTICE-HALL OF AUSTRALIA, PTY. LTD., Sydney
PRENTICE-HALL OF CANADA, LTD., Toronto
PRENTICE-HALL OF INDIA PRIVATE LIMITED, New Delhi
PRENTICE-HALL OF JAPAN, INC., Tokyo

Foreword

The Central Issues in Philosophy series is based upon the conviction that the best way to teach philosophy to introductory students is to experience or to *do* philosophy with them. The basic unit of philosophical investigation is the particular problem, and not the area or the historical figure. Therefore, this series consists of sets of readings organised around well-defined, manageable problems. All other things being equal, problems that are of interest and relevance to the student have been chosen.

Each volume contains an introduction that clearly defines the problem and sets out the alternative positions that have been taken. The selections are chosen and arranged in such a way as to take the student through the dialectic of the problem; each reading, besides presenting a particular point of view, criticizes the points of view set out earlier.

Although no attempt has been made to introduce the student in a systematic way to the history of philosophy, classical selections relevant to the development of the problem have been included. As a side benefit, the student will therefore come to see the continuity, as well as the breaks, between classical and contemporary thought. But in no case will a selection be included merely for its historical significance; clarity of expression and systematic significance are the main criteria for selection.

BARUCH A. BRODY

Contents

Introduction

The famous attorney Clarence Darrow once addressed the prisoners in the Cook County Jail as follows:

> There is no such thing as a crime as the word is generally understood. I do not believe there is any sort of distinction between the real moral conditions of the people in and out of jail. One is just as good as the other. The people here can no more help being here than the people outside can avoid being outside. I do not believe that people are in jail because they deserve to be. They are in jail simply because they cannot avoid it on account of circumstances which are entirely beyond their control and for which they are in no way responsible. . . . There are people who think that everything in this world is an accident. But really there is no such thing as an accident. . . . There are a great many people here who have done some of these things [murder, theft, *etc.*] who really do not know themselves why they did them. It looked to you at the time as if you had a chance to do them or not, as you saw fit; but still, after all you had no choice. . . . If you look at the question deeply enough and carefully enough you will see that there were circumstances that drove you to do exactly the thing which you did. You could not help it any more than we outside can help taking the positions that we take.

This is an excellent, if somewhat extreme, statement of a view held by many people regarding the implications of a thesis about the nature of the world which may be called *determinism*. This view has

1

its roots in the earliest attempts to grasp in a rational manner some understanding of the universe, and it remains today a point of controversy among theoretical physicists. It is a philosophical issue which, as the quotation from Darrow illustrates, professes to have important implications for the ways in which we think, talk, and act. This collection of articles is an attempt to introduce to a beginning student of philosophy the problem of determinism and free will.

I

There are basically three questions that can be asked of any philosophical thesis: What does it mean? Is it true? What difference does it make? The organization of this book reflects these questions, as will this introduction.

II

It is by no means easy to define the thesis of determinism in any very precise manner. And the definition of the thesis will determine its implications. If, for example, one defines determinism as "the denial of free will," whatever the latter might be, then it will be a logical truth that if determinism is true, there is no free will. But this way of proceeding, although it has what Bertrand Russell calls "the advantages of theft over honest toil," will not prove intellectually satisfying. If possible one would like a definition of the thesis which meets the following requirements: (1) It does not beg any questions concerning the important implications of the thesis; (2) It does not involve any terms which are at least as problematic as the one being defined; and (3) The thesis seems to have some chance of being true.

The usual model on which a definition is constructed is the kind of knowledge gained by the physical sciences. The classical view as stated by the eighteenth-century mathematician Laplace is that "an intelligence knowing all the forces acting in nature at a given instant, as well as the momentary positions of all things in the universe, would be able to comprehend in one single formula the motions of the largest bodies as well as the lightest atoms. . . . To it nothing would be uncertain, the future as well as the past would be present to its eyes." [1] This statement contains the two fundamental ingredients of any determinism: a belief in universal causal laws and a notion of predictability. Although it is the feature of predictability that has usually been stressed, perhaps because psychologically that is the feature of determinism that bothers people, it is really the presence of causal laws and explanations which characterizes the determinist position. As soon as it is pointed out to the determinist that as a matter of fact he cannot predict, for example, the next three words I am going to write, he falls back on a notion of *predictable-in-principle*. But the only basis for believing that such predictions are in principle possible is the premise that there are causal factors at work determining the future in a unique fashion, such factors being in principle capable of being known. It is, however, possible that the world may be a deterministic system, although its complexity might be such that we could not grasp the causal laws involved and hence could not use them in making predictions.

How then shall we formulate the deterministic thesis? Let us consider some given system. It might be a human being or an amoeba or a television set or the solar system. Certain things happen to the system, and it, in turn, does certain things. In scientific jargon, there are inputs and outputs. In addition the system has a certain internal structure of its own. The determinist asserts that the output of the system is a unique function of the input and the internal structure. Given any output, O, there are universally true causal laws which determine O uniquely on the basis of the internal structure of the system and some of the inputs. For every output O there were earlier events which were sufficient for the production of O. That is, if we could now move backwards in time to some earlier point and we kept all the variables of the system at the same values they had at the earlier time, then the system would again produce O as its output. Now determinism asserts that the universe is just such a deterministic system, and it then of course follows that the particular systems we call human beings are deterministic systems.

Determinism should not be confused with what might be called predeterminism, or *fatalism*. Fatalism states that our output is not

---

[1] Laplace, *Théorie Analytique des Probabilités* (2nd ed.), (Paris, 1814), p. ii.

affected by any efforts or decisions that we make. This is a stronger claim than determinism, in effect not only claiming that our outputs are caused, but also specifying certain factors as being causally irrelevant to the outcome. This thesis suffers from the defect that there is no reason to suppose it true and every reason to regard it as false.

From the intuitive and rough characterization given above we may try and produce more precise formulations. For example: For any event E

1. The occurrence of E was causally necessitated
2. The occurrence of E has a sufficient explanation in causal terms
3. E had sufficient antecedent conditions
4. The occurrence of E was in principle predictable
5. There exist a set of events, C, and a true law of nature, L, which asserts that if C were to occur then E would occur.

We may then define *indeterminism* as the negation of determinism, that is, as the view that there is at least one event E of which the defining conditions for determinism do not hold.

We now see emerging that circle of concepts which encloses the problem: cause, necessity, sufficient conditions, causal explanation, predictability, law of nature. Explaining and clarifying these concepts is one of the main tasks of the philosopher.

III

Given some understanding of the thesis, we can then address ourselves to the existence of evidence for its truth. Why should anyone ever have supposed that the universe is a deterministic system? And are there good reasons for such a belief? The answer to these questions depends on how the thesis is to be construed. Is it supposed to be, for example, just a broad generalization from experience? A child might find that if he drops a ball it falls toward the floor. He then might discover that this is true for all of his toys—balloons excepted. Perhaps then he would observe that this property holds true no matter which room of his house he is in and indeed everywhere he goes. Next he could conjecture that (almost) all objects anywhere on earth fall if left unsupported. His generalization could then be extended to the entire universe. One difficulty with treating determinism in an analogous fashion as an inductive generalization is that if a proposition is a generalization from experience it should be possible to find it false on the basis of further experience. But it is not clear how to do this with the deterministic thesis, for the failure to find causal laws governing the occurrence of any given event does not mean there are none; the determinist can always ask us to look further. Of course, sometimes the best reason for supposing something does not exist is that we have looked very carefully and extensively and have not found it to exist. But sometimes the reasoning for supposing something not to exist will be of a more theoretical nature. The reason I do not believe in the existence of a man who can fly by flapping his arms is not that I have made a thorough search for such a creature and failed to find one, but that on the basis of a well-confirmed anatomical and physical theory there cannot be such a creature. Although there have been few attempts by indeterminists to use such reasoning to show that there are (must be) uncaused events, one such line of reasoning is to be found in the selection by Peirce.

Nagel, on the other hand, does not construe the thesis to be an empirical one but rather interprets it as a regulative principle or postulate, to be judged on its fruitful consequences for scientific investigation of the world. The reader must judge for himself how successful this approach is and whether it avoids Peirce's ironic onslaught.

Finally there are attempts such as Hume's to show that belief in determinism is warranted as the only way in which we can account for the judgments and predictions we make about the behavior of our fellow men. What has to be shown by this line of argument is that we do use a principle as strong as the determinist principle to make judgments, and further that we cannot arrive at the same results by using any weaker theory, that is, one that only assumes that *most* events are determined uniquely or one that makes use of only statistical determinations.

IV

Let us turn now to the issue of *free will*. How is it to be defined? And what are the logical connections between free will and determinism? The intuitive idea underlying the notion of free will is that of an openness of possibilities for the agent. It is commonly believed that although, as a matter of fact, a man did one thing rather than another—for example, went to the movies rather than watch television—it was open to him to have done something else instead. There were alternatives to his action which were genuine possibilities. Similarly, it is commonly believed that at present there are various possibilities which I can bring about. I can either continue writing or stop, decide to pay my income tax or refuse to pay, lift my arm or keep it at my side. The claim that we have free will is, then, the claim that for some actions at least the following condition is true: There is an alternative action (which may be simply refraining from the action to be performed) open to the agent. Put in the past tense after the agent has performed some action A: There was some alternative action which the agent could have performed other than the one which he in fact did.

Both Campbell and Reid attempt to show the truth of this thesis on the basis of appeals to introspective evidence. Reid takes the more cautious line, trying to show that a careful examination of our inner experience produces enough evidence at least to throw the burden of proof on anyone denying free will. The DeValla and Herbst articles are interesting attempts to understand the connection between the possibility of others (including God) making correct and justified predictions about our future actions and the concept of free will.

There are three possible positions than can be taken with respect to the relation between determinism and free will: (1) determinism is inconsistent with free will—that is, the truth of determinism entails the falsity of free will; (2) the truth of determinism entails the truth of free will; or (3) the two positions are logically independent —that is, nothing follows about the truth or falsity of free will from the truth of determinism. For the sake of symmetry, and because there is little reason to suppose (2) is true, (2) and (3) are usually lumped together as the claim that determinism and free will are compatible or consistent, while (1) is the belief that the two theses are inconsistent.

Most of the fuss over this subject has arisen because it has seemed obvious to many philosophers that determinism is inconsistent with free will. Here is a typical argument: Suppose I were faced with a choice between vanilla and chocolate ice cream, and I chose vanilla. Could I have chosen chocolate? If determinism is true, then we can find some causal law linking the choice I made with antecedent conditions such as my upbringing, my tastes, my moods, and so forth. But if the law is true, and if the initial conditions are present, then the law plus initial conditions will entail that this choice and no other takes place. It would be contradictory to admit whenever A, then B, and then to admit A and reject B. If there were indeed sufficient conditions for my choice of vanilla ice cream, then I could not have chosen chocolate ice cream, for then the conditions must not have been sufficient, but at most perhaps necessary. It is no more possible for me to choose chocolate than for a piece of paper to turn to ice when a blow-torch is applied to it.

Those philosophers who have wished to resist this conclusion, to show that determinism and free will are consistent, have proceeded by arguing that words such as "can," "would have," and "possible" are not self-evident terms, and that a proper analysis would show that, correctly understood, I could have chosen differently even if determinism is true. Determinism and free will seem to be inconsistent only because we think that "I could have done otherwise" means "I could have done otherwise in exactly those circumstances in which I did not do otherwise." But, it is suggested, what should be understood by this phrase is, roughly, "I could have done otherwise if such-and-such had been the case (I had chosen differently, I had tried harder, I had had a different upbringing, *etc.*)." The Hume and Moore selections illustrate this approach to the problem.

The reply to this line of argument, as the Broad and Lehrer articles illustrate, is that although this may be one meaning that the phrase "could have done otherwise" may carry, it is not the sense that this phrase must bear if we are to justify our ordinary ways of judging people blameworthy and punishing them. For this we must have a categorical sense of possibility rather than a hypothetical sense. Not "could have done otherwise" *if*, but "could have done otherwise," period.

At this point in the debate it becomes clear that the question of the proper analysis of the notions of "possibility," "could have done otherwise," and so forth, must be tied in with a conception of the puzzles and problems being raised. Determinism is widely supposed to undermine many commonly held beliefs about human responsibility, and the thesis of free will is supposed to rescue us from this quandary.

The following argument attempts to develop the above implications:

1. A necessary condition for holding a person responsible, blaming, or punishing him for an act, A, is that the person did A freely.
2. If determinism is true nobody ever acts freely.
3. Therefore, if determinism is true, no one is ever responsible, blameworthy, or punishable.
4. At least sometimes agents are responsible, blameworthy, or punishable for what they do.
5. Therefore, determinism is false.

To return to the question of the compatibility of free will and determinism, that is, whether premise (2) in the above argument is true, we can now define the problem more accurately. What sense of "acting freely" or "could have done otherwise" is required by premise (1), and is determinism consistent with *that* sense of the term?

Determinists who wish to hold onto our common belief that sometimes we are responsible for what we do analyze the notion of responsibility in such a way that it is consistent with a hypothetical analysis of "could have done otherwise,"—"would have done otherwise, if. . . ." This analysis of responsibility is usually some form of what might be called a "modifiability" theory. According to this theory, a person is morally responsible for an action if and only if he is modifiable by blame and punishment. A wrongdoer is morally responsible if and only if punishment would have affected his choice to do something wrong in the past or will now influence him to avoid such actions in the future. Hence we need a sense of "could have done otherwise" which is relevant to the modifiability of the agent. Now a hypothetical analysis in terms of choice looks plausible. For in those cases where the agent could have done otherwise if he had so chosen, and if his choices in the future will be influenced by blame or punishment, we are justified in holding him responsible, blaming him, and so forth.

Those who insist that the "can" needed is a categorical one, and hence that premise (2) is true, argue that the equation of moral responsibility with modifiability is mistaken and has absurd consequences, that the notions of blame and punishment have other than utilitarian justifications, and that the reason we insist on a "could have done otherwise" condition is not that we are interested in changing behavior but that we are interested in being fair. And it is not simply inefficacious to punish a man who could not have done otherwise (sometimes, indeed it may be efficacious); it is unjust. We are inflicting sanctions (formal or informal) on a man who could not have avoided his wrong conduct. By parody of reasoning, so it is argued, the hypothetical analysis of "could have done otherwise" should apply to a man in a coma; for surely he could have or even would have saved a drowning child if he had so chosen.

There is an interesting parallel between the way in which philosophers in the British empiricist tradition (Locke, Hume, Mill) treat the problem of free will and the way in which they analyze the issue of social freedom or liberty. In both cases freedom is defined, roughly, as being able to do what one wishes or chooses to do. And in both cases the feeling is that pushing the inquiry further into the conditions under which people have acquired the desires they have is unnecessary and illegitimate. Thus for the social freedom theorist, the question of whether or not members of a society have been indoctrinated, manipulated, or brainwashed into certain needs or desires is irrelevant to issues of liberty. As long as they have those desires and are able to act to satisfy them, they are free men. The parallel argument for free will is that it does not matter whether or not a man's choices have causal antecedents. All that is important is that if he should choose or desire otherwise he would be able to translate those desires and choices into action. In both cases opponents have argued that, although this initial definition is part of the story of freedom, it is merely a part, and that it would be a mockery to insist that a man is free with all the implications of that assessment unless that portion of the story which involves the determinants of a man's choices is brought in as well.

The articles by Smart, Broad, Moore, Thomas, and Lehrer discuss the proper analysis of "could have done otherwise" and its implications for questions of *moral responsibility*.

V

There has been more sympathy in recent years for the view that determinism is inconsistent with free will and has radical implications for our moral outlook upon the world. If we are to make progress on this problem we must take determinism seriously and not assume that it leaves everything as it is. But even if this position is accepted, it is not enough to argue that because we all believe people are often responsible for their conduct determinism is false. Our intuitions on this matter might have to give way before the theory rather than *vice versa*. Still, if anything will work, it is this type of strategy. Determinism, like most philosophical theses, will not fall to any single attack or knock-down argument. Rather it must be undermined in as many different ways as we have imagination and ingenuity to conceive. It is only by revealing as many counterintuitive results as possible, covering as broad a range of thought about human beings as possible, that we can successfully dislodge a mistaken view.

Determinists—historically often persons most interested and concerned with human freedom (Spinoza, Marx, Freud)—have assumed that the only things that would disappear as a result of accepting their views are vengeance, vindictiveness, smug views of moral superiority, and so forth. What has to be shown is that the consequences are far more drastic, that the entire notion of a human agent disappears as well.

WHAT IS DETERMINISM AND IS IT TRUE?

DAVID HUME

Of Liberty and Necessity

※ ※

PART I

It might reasonably be expected in questions which have been canvassed and disputed with great eagerness, since the first origin of science and philosophy, that the meaning of all the terms, at least, should have been agreed upon among the disputants; and our enquiries, in the course of two thousand years, been able to pass from words to the true and real subject of the controversy. For how easy may it seem to give exact definitions of the terms employed in reasoning, and make these definitions, not the mere sound of words, the object of future scrutiny and examination? But if we consider the matter more narrowly, we shall be apt to draw a quite opposite conclusion. From this circumstance alone, that a controversy has been long kept on foot, and remains still undecided, we may presume that there is some ambiguity in the expression, and that the disputants affix different ideas to the terms employed in the controversy. For as the faculties of the mind are supposed to be naturally alike in every individual; otherwise nothing could be more fruitless than to reason or dispute together; it were impossible, if men affix the same ideas to their terms, that they could so long form different opinions of the same subject; especially when they communicate their views, and each party turn themselves on all sides, in search of arguments which may give them the victory over their antagonists. It is true, if men

---

* From David Hume, *An Inquiry Concerning Human Understanding*, Sec. 8.

attempt the discussion of questions which lie entirely beyond the reach of human capacity, such as those concerning the origin of worlds, or the economy of the intellectual system or region of spirits, they may long beat the air in their fruitless contests, and never arrive at any determinate conclusion. But if the question regard any subject of common life and experience, nothing, one would think, could preserve the dispute so long undecided but some ambiguous expressions, which keep the antagonists still at a distance, and hinder them from grappling with each other.

This has been the case in the long disputed question concerning liberty and necessity; and to so remarkable a degree that, if I be not much mistaken, we shall find, that all mankind, both learned and ignorant, have always been of the same opinion with regard to this subject, and that a few intelligible definitions would immediately have put an end to the whole controversy. I own that this dispute has been so much canvassed on all hands, and has led philosophers into such a labyrinth of obscure sophistry, that it is no wonder, if a sensible reader indulge his ease so far as to turn a deaf ear to the proposal of such a question, from which he can expect neither instruction or entertainment. But the state of the argument here proposed may, perhaps, serve to renew his attention; as it has more novelty, promises at least some decision of the controversy, and will not much disturb his ease by any intricate or obscure reasoning.

I hope, therefore, to make it appear that all men have ever agreed in the doctrine both of necessity and of liberty, according to any reasonable sense, which can be put on these terms; and that the whole controversy has hitherto turned merely upon words. We shall begin with examining the doctrine of necessity.

It is universally allowed that matter, in all its operations, is actuated by a necessary force, and that every natural effect is so precisely determined by the energy of its cause that no other effect, in such particular circumstances, could possibly have resulted from it. The degree and direction of every motion is, by the laws of nature, prescribed with such exactness that a living creature may as soon arise from the shock of two bodies as motion in any other degree or direction than what is actually produced by it. Would we, therefore, form a just and precise idea of *necessity,* we must consider whence that idea arises when we apply it to the operation of bodies.

It seems evident that, if all the scenes of nature were continually shifted in such a manner that no two events bore any resemblance to each other, but every object was entirely new, without any similitude to whatever had been seen before, we should never, in that case, have attained the least idea of necessity, or of a connexion among these objects. We might say, upon such a supposition, that one object or event has followed another; not that one was produced by the other. The relation of cause and effect must be utterly unknown to mankind. Inference and reasoning concerning the operations of nature would, from that moment, be at an end; and the memory and senses remain the only canals, by which the knowledge of any real existence could possibly have access to the mind. Our idea, therefore, of necessity and causation arises entirely from the uniformity observable in the operations of nature, where similar objects are constantly conjoined together, and the mind is determined by custom to infer the one from the appearance of the other. These two circumstances form the whole of that necessity, which we ascribe to matter. Beyond the constant *conjunction* of similar objects, and the consequent *inference* from one to the other, we have no notion of any necessity or connexion.

If it appear, therefore, that all mankind have ever allowed, without any doubt or hesitation, that these two circumstances take place in the voluntary actions of men, and in the operations of mind; it must follow, that all mankind have ever agreed in the doctrine of necessity, and that they have hitherto disputed, merely for not understanding each other.

As to the first circumstance, the constant and regular conjunction of similar events, we may possibly satisfy ourselves by the following considerations. It is universally acknowledged that there is a great uniformity among the actions of men, in all nations and ages, and that human nature remains still the same, in its principles and operations. The same motives always produce the same actions: The same events follow from the same causes. Ambition, avarice, self-love, vanity, friendship, generosity, public spirit: these passions, mixed in various degrees, and distributed through society, have been, from the beginning of the world, and still are, the source of all the actions and enterprises, which have ever been observed among mankind. Would you know the sentiments, inclinations, and course of life of the Greeks and Romans? Study well the temper and actions of the French and English: You cannot be much mistaken in transferring to the former *most* of the observations which you have made with regard to the latter. Mankind are so much the same, in all times and places, that history informs us of nothing new or strange in this particular. Its chief use is only to discover the constant and universal principles of human nature, by showing men in all varieties of circumstances and situations, and furnishing us with materials from which we may form our observations and become acquainted with the regular springs of human action and behaviour. These records of wars, intrigues, factions, and revolutions, are so many collections of experiments, by which the politician or moral philosopher fixes the principles of his science, in the same manner as the physician or natural philosopher becomes acquainted with the nature of plants, minerals, and other external objects, by the experiments which he forms concerning them. Nor are the earth, water, and other elements, examined by Aristotle, and Hippocrates, more like to those which at present lie under our observation than the men described by Polybius and Tacitus are to those who now govern the world.

Should a traveller, returning from a far country, bring us an account of men, wholly different from any with whom we were ever acquainted; men, who were entirely divested of avarice, ambition, or revenge; who knew no pleasure but friendship, generosity, and public spirit; we should immediately, from these circumstances, detect the falsehood, and prove him a liar, with the same certainty as if he had stuffed his narration with stories of centaurs and dragons, miracles and prodigies. And if we would explode any forgery in history, we cannot make use of a more convincing argument, than to prove, that the actions ascribed to any person are directly contrary to the course of nature, and that no human motives, in such circumstances, could ever induce him to such a conduct. The veracity of Quintus Curtius is as much to be suspected, when he describes the supernatural courage of Alexander, by which he was hurried on singly to attack multitudes, as when he describes his supernatural force and activity, by which he was able to resist them. So readily and universally do we acknowledge a uniformity in human motives and actions as well as in the operations of body.

Hence likewise the benefit of that experience, acquired by long life and a variety of business and company, in order to instruct us in the principles of human nature, and regulate our future conduct, as well as speculation. By means of this guide, we mount up to the knowledge of men's inclinations and motives, from their actions, expressions, and even gestures; and again descend to the interpretation of their actions from our knowledge of their motives and inclinations. The general observations treasured up by a course of experience, give us the clue of human nature, and teach us to unravel all its intricacies. Pretexts and appearances no longer deceive us. Public declarations pass for the specious colouring of a cause. And though virtue and honour be allowed their proper weight and authority, that perfect disinterestedness, so often pretended to, is never expected in multitudes and parties; seldom in their leaders; and scarcely even in individuals of any rank or station. But were there no uniformity in human actions, and were every experiment which we could form of this kind irregular and anomalous, it were impossible to collect any general observations concerning mankind; and no experience, however accurately digested by reflection, would ever serve to any purpose. Why is the aged husbandman more skilful in his calling than the young beginner but because there is a certain uniformity in the operation of the sun, rain, and earth towards the production of vegetables; and experience teaches the old practitioner the rules by which this operation is governed and directed.

We must not, however, expect that this uniformity of human actions should be carried to such a length as that all men, in the same circumstances, will always act precisely in the same manner, without making any allowance for the diversity of characters, prejudices, and opinions. Such a uniformity in every particular, is found in no part of nature. On the contrary, from observing the variety of conduct in different men, we are enabled to form a greater variety of maxims, which still suppose a degree of uniformity and regularity.

Are the manners of men different in different ages and countries? We learn thence the great force of custom and education, which mould the human mind from its infancy and form it into a fixed and established character. Is the behaviour and conduct of the one sex very unlike that of the other? Is it thence we become acquainted with the different characters which nature has impressed upon the sexes, and which she preserves with constancy and regularity? Are the actions of the same person much diversified in the different periods of his life, from infancy to old age? This affords room for many general observations concerning the gradual change of our sentiments and inclinations, and the different maxims which prevail in the different ages of human creatures. Even the characters, which are peculiar to each individual, have a uniformity in their influence; otherwise our acquaintance with the persons and our observation of their conduct could never teach us their dispositions, or serve to direct our behaviour with regard to them.

I grant it possible to find some actions, which seem to have no regular connexion with any known motives, and are exceptions to all the measures of conduct which have ever been established for the government of men. But if we would willingly know what judgement should be formed of such irregular and extraordinary actions, we may consider the sentiments commonly entertained with regard to those irregular events which appear in the course of nature, and the operations of external objects. All causes are not conjoined to their usual effects with like uniformity. An artificer, who handles only dead matter, may be disappointed of his aim, as well as the politician, who directs the conduct of sensible and intelligent agents.

The vulgar, who take things according to their first appearance, attribute the uncertainty of events to such an uncertainty in the causes as makes the latter often fail of their usual influence; though they meet with no impediment in their operation. But philosophers, observing that, almost in every part of nature, there is contained a vast variety of springs and principles, which are hid, by reason of their minuteness or remoteness, find, that it is at least possible the contrariety of events may not proceed from any contingency in the cause, but from the secret operation of contrary causes. This possibility is converted into certainty by farther observation, when they remark that, upon an exact scrutiny, a contrariety of effects always betrays a contrariety of causes, and proceeds from their mutual opposition. A peasant can give no better reason for the stopping of any clock or watch than to say that it does not commonly go right: But an artist easily perceives that the same force in the spring or pendulum has always the same influence on the wheels; but fails of its usual effect, perhaps by reason of a grain of dust, which puts a stop to the whole movement. From the observation of several parallel instances, philosophers form a maxim that the connexion between all causes and effects is equally necessary, and that its seeming uncertainty in some instances proceeds from the secret opposition of contrary causes.

Thus, for instance, in the human body, when the usual symptoms of health or sickness disappoint our expectation; when medicines operate not with their wonted powers; when irregular events follow from any particular cause; the philosopher and physician are not surprised at the matter, nor are ever tempted to deny, in general, the necessity and uniformity of those principles by which the animal economy is conducted. They know that a human body is a mighty complicated machine: That many secret powers lurk in it, which are altogether beyond our comprehension: That to us it must often appear very uncertain in its operations: And that therefore the irregular events, which outwardly discover themselves, can be no proof that the laws of nature are not observed with the greatest regularity in its internal operations and government.

The philosopher, if he be consistent, must apply the same reasoning to the actions and volitions of intelligent agents. The most irregular and unexpected resolutions of men may frequently be accounted for by those who know every particular circumstance of their character and situation. A person of an obliging disposition gives a peevish answer: But he has the toothache, or has not dined. A stupid fellow discovers an uncommon alacrity in his carriage: But he has met with a sudden piece of good fortune. Or even when an action, as sometimes happens, cannot be particularly accounted for, either by the person himself or by others; we know, in general, that the characters of men are, to a certain degree, inconstant and irregular. This is, in a manner, the constant character of human nature; though it be applicable, in a more particular manner, to some persons who have no fixed rule for their conduct, but proceed in a continued course of caprice and inconstancy. The internal principles and motives may operate in a uniform manner, notwithstanding these seeming irregularities; in the same manner as the winds, rain, clouds, and other variations of the weather are supposed to be governed by steady principles; though not easily discoverable by human sagacity and enquiry.

Thus it appears, not only that the conjunction between motives and voluntary actions is as regular and uniform as that between the cause and effect in any part of nature; but also that this regular conjunction has been universally acknowledged among mankind, and has never been the subject of dispute, either in philosophy or common life. Now, as it is from past experience that we draw all inferences concerning the future, and as we conclude that objects will always be conjoined together which we find to have always been conjoined; it may seem superfluous to prove that this experienced uniformity in human actions is a source whence we draw *inferences* concerning them. But in order to throw the argument into a greater variety of lights we shall also insist, though briefly, on this latter topic.

The mutual dependence of men is so great in all societies that scarce any human action is entirely complete in itself, or is performed without some reference to the actions of others, which are requisite to make it answer fully the intention of the agent. The poorest artificer, who labours alone, expects at least the protection of the magistrate, to ensure him the enjoyment of the fruits of his labour. He also expects that, when he carries his goods to market, and offers them at a reasonable price, he shall find purchasers, and shall be able, by the money he acquires, to engage others to supply him with those commodities which are requisite for his subsistence. In proportion as men extend their dealings, and render their intercourse with others more complicated, they always comprehend, in their schemes of life, a greater variety of voluntary actions, which they expect, from the proper motives, to cooperate with their own. In all these conclusions they take their measures from past experience, in the same manner as in their reasonings concerning external objects; and firmly believe that men, as well as all the elements, are to continue, in their operations, the same that they have ever found them. A manufacturer reckons upon the labour of his servants for the execution of any work as much as upon the tools which he employs, and would be equally surprised were his expectations disappointed. In short, this experimental inference and reasoning concerning the actions of others enters so much into human life that no man, while awake, is ever a moment without employing it. Have we not reason, therefore, to affirm that all mankind have always agreed in the doctrine of necessity according to the foregoing definition and explication of it?

Nor have philosophers ever entertained a different opinion from the people in this particular. For, not to mention that almost every action of their life supposes that opinion, there are even few of the speculative parts of learning to which it is not essential. What would become of *history*, had we not a dependence on the veracity of the historian according to the experience which we have had of mankind? How could *politics* be a science, if laws and forms of government had not a uniform influence upon society? Where would be the foundation of *morals*, if particular characters had no certain or determinate power to produce particular sentiments, and if these sentiments had no constant operation on actions? And with what pretence could we employ our *criticism* upon any poet or polite author, if we could not pronounce the conduct and sentiments of his actors either natural or unnatural to such characters, and in such circumstances? It seems almost impossible, therefore, to engage either in science or action of any kind without acknowledging the doctrine of necessity, and this *inference* from motive to voluntary actions, from characters to conduct.

And indeed, when we consider how aptly *natural* and *moral* evidence link together, and form only one chain of argument, we shall make no scruple to allow that they are of the same nature, and derived from the same principles. A prisoner who has neither money nor interest, discovers the impossibility of his escape, as well when he considers the obstinacy of the gaoler, as the walls and bars with which he is surrounded; and, in all attempts for his freedom, chooses rather to work upon the stone and iron of the one, than upon the inflexible nature of the other. The same prisoner, when conducted to the scaffold, foresees his death as certainly from the constancy and fidelity of his guards, as from the operation of the axe or wheel. His mind runs along a certain train of ideas: The refusal of the soldiers to consent to his escape; the action of the executioner; the separation of the head and body; bleeding, convulsive motions, and death. Here is a connected chain of natural causes and voluntary actions; but the mind feels no difference between them in passing from one link to another: Nor is less certain of the future event than if it were connected with the objects present to the memory or senses, by a train of causes, cemented together by what we are pleased to call a *physical* necessity. The same experienced union has the same effect on the mind, whether the united objects be motives, volition, and actions; or figure and motion. We may change the name of things; but their nature and their operation on the understanding never change.

Were a man, whom I know to be honest and opulent, and with whom I live in intimate friendship, to come into my house, where I am surrounded with my servants, I rest assured that he is not to stab me before he leaves it in order to rob me of my silver standish; and I no more suspect this event than the falling of the house itself, which is new, and solidly built and founded. *But he may have been seized with a sudden and unknown frenzy.* So may a sudden earthquake arise, and shake and tumble my house about my ears. I shall therefore change the suppositions. I shall say that I know with certainty that he is not to put his hand into the fire and hold it there till it be consumed: And this event, I think I can foretell with the same assurance, as that, if he throw himself out at the window, and meet with no obstruction, he will not remain a moment suspended in the air. No suspicion of an unknown frenzy can give the least possibility to the former event, which is so contrary to all the known principles of human nature. A man who at noon leaves his purse full of gold on the pavement at Charing-Cross, may as well expect that it will fly away like a feather, as that he will find it untouched an hour after. Above one half of human reasonings contain inferences of a similar nature, attended with more or less degrees of certainty proportioned to our experience of the usual conduct of mankind in such particular situations.

I have frequently considered, what could possibly be the reason why all mankind, though they have ever, without hesitation, acknowledged the doctrine of necessity in their whole practice and reasoning, have yet discovered such a reluctance to acknowledge it in words, and have rather shown a propensity, in all ages, to profess the contrary opinion. The matter, I think, may be accounted for after the following manner. If we examine the operations of body, and the production of effects from their causes, we shall find that all our faculties can never carry us farther in our knowledge of this relation than barely to observe that particular objects are *constantly conjoined* together, and that the mind is carried, by a *customary transition,* from the appearance of one to the belief of the other. But though this conclusion concerning human ignorance be the result of the strictest scrutiny of this subject, men still entertain a strong propensity to believe that they penetrate farther into the powers of nature, and perceive something like a necessary connexion between the cause and the effect. When again they turn their reflections towards the operations of their own minds, and *feel* no such connexion of the motive and the action; they are thence apt to suppose, that there is a difference between the effects which result from material force, and those which arise from thought and intelligence. But being once convinced that we know nothing farther of causation of any kind than merely the *constant conjunction* of objects, and the consequent *inference* of the mind from one to another, and finding that these two circumstances are universally allowed to have place in voluntary actions; we may be more easily led to own the same necessity common to all causes. And though this reasoning may contradict the systems of many philosophers, in ascribing necessity to the determinations of the will, we shall find, upon reflection, that they dissent from it in words only, not in their real sentiment. Necessity, according to the sense in which it is here taken, has never yet been rejected, nor can ever, I think, be rejected by any philosopher. It may only, perhaps, be pretended that the mind can perceive, in the operations of matter, some farther connexion between the cause and effect; and connexion that has not place in voluntary actions of intelligent beings. Now whether it be so or not, can only appear upon examination; and it is incumbent on these philosophers to make good their assertion, by defining or describing that necessity, and pointing it out to us in the operations of material causes.

It would seem, indeed, that men begin at the wrong end of this question concerning liberty and necessity, when they enter upon it by examining the faculties of the soul, the influence of the understanding, and the operations of the will. Let them first discuss a more simple question, namely, the operations of body and of brute unintelligent matter; and try whether they can there form any idea of causation and necessity, except that of a constant conjunction of objects, and subsequent inference of the mind from one to another. If these circumstances form, in reality, the whole of that necessity, which we conceive in matter, and if these circumstances be also universally acknowledged to take place in the operations of the mind, the dispute is at an end; at least, must be owned to be thenceforth merely verbal. But as long as we will rashly suppose, that we have some farther idea of necessity and causation in the operations of external objects; at the same time, that we can find nothing farther in the voluntary actions of the mind; there is no possibility of bringing the question to any determinate issue, while we proceed upon so erroneous a supposition. The only method of undeceiving us is to mount up higher; to examine the narrow extent of science when applied to material causes; and to convince ourselves that all we know of them is the constant conjunction and inference above mentioned. We may, perhaps, find that it is with difficulty we are induced to fix such narrow limits to human understanding: But we can afterwards find no difficulty when we come to apply this doctrine to the actions of the will. For as it is evident that these have a regular conjunction with motives and circumstances and characters, and as we always draw inferences from one to the other, we must be obliged to acknowledge in words that necessity, which we have already avowed, in every deliberation of our lives, and in every step of our conduct and behaviour.[1]

[1] The prevalence of the doctrine of liberty may be accounted for, from another cause, *viz.* a false sensation or seeming experience which we have, or may have, of liberty or indifference, in many of our actions. The necessity of any action, whether of matter or of mind, is not, properly speaking, a quality in the agent, but in any thinking or intelligent being, who may consider the action; and it consists chiefly in the determination of his thoughts to infer the existence of that action from some preceding objects; as liberty, when opposed to necessity, is nothing but the want of that determination, and a certain looseness or indifference, which we feel, in passing, or not passing, from the idea of one object to that of any succeeding one. Now we may observe that, though, in *reflecting* on human actions, we seldom feel such a looseness, or indifference, but are commonly able to infer them with considerable certainty from their motives, and from the dispositions of the agent; yet it frequently happens, that, in *performing* the actions themselves, we are sensible of something like it: And as all resembling objects are readily taken for each other, this has been employed as a demonstrative and even intuitive proof of human liberty. We feel, that our actions are subject to our will, on most occasions; and imagine we feel, that the will itself is subject to nothing, because, when by a denial of it we are provoked to try, we feel, that it moves easily every way, and produces an image of itself (or a *Velleïty*, as it is called in the schools) even on that side, on which it did not settle. This image, or faint motion, we persuade ourselves, could, at that time, have been compleated into the thing itself; because, should that be denied, we

But to proceed in this reconciling project with regard to the question of liberty and necessity; the most contentious question of metaphysics, the most contentious science; it will not require many words to prove, that all mankind have ever agreed in the doctrine of liberty as well as in that of necessity, and that the whole dispute, in this respect also, has been hitherto merely verbal. For what is meant by liberty, when applied to voluntary actions? We cannot surely mean that actions have so little connexion with motives, inclinations, and circumstances, that one does not follow with a certain degree of uniformity from the other, and that one affords no inference by which we can conclude the existence of the other. For these are plain and acknowledged matters of fact. By liberty, then, we can only mean *a power of acting or not acting, according to the determinations of the will;* that is, if we choose to remain at rest, we may; if we choose to move, we also may. Now this hypothetical liberty is universally allowed to belong to everyone who is not a prisoner and in chains. Here, then, is no subject of dispute.

Whatever definition we may give of liberty, we should be careful to observe two requisite circumstances; *first,* that it be consistent with plain matter of fact; *secondly,* that it be consistent with itself. If we observe these circumstances, and render our definition intelligible, I am persuaded that all mankind will be found of one opinion with regard to it.

It is universally allowed that nothing exists without a cause of its existence, and that chance, when strictly examined, is a mere negative word, and means not any real power which has anywhere a being in nature. But it is pretended that some causes are necessary, some not necessary. Here then is the advantage of definitions. Let any one *define* a cause, without comprehending, as a part of the definition, a *necessary connexion* with its effect; and let him show

---

find, upon a second trial, that, at present, it can. We consider not, that the fantastical desire of shewing liberty, is here the motive of our actions. And it seems certain, that, however we may imagine we feel a liberty within ourselves, a spectator can commonly infer our actions from our motives and character; and even where he cannot, he concludes in general, that he might, were he perfectly acquainted with every circumstance of our situation and temper, and the most secret springs of our complexion and disposition. Now this is the very essence of necessity, according to the foregoing doctrine.

distinctly the origin of the idea, expressed by the definition; and I shall readily give up the whole controversy. But if the foregoing explication of the matter be received, this must be absolutely impracticable. Had not objects a regular conjunction with each other, we should never have entertained any notion of cause and effect; and this regular conjunction produces that inference of the understanding, which is the only connexion, that we can have any comprehension of. Whoever attempts a definition of cause, exclusive of these circumstances, will be obliged either to employ unintelligible terms or such as are synonymous to the term which he endeavours to define.[2] And if the definition above mentioned be admitted; liberty, when opposed to necessity, not to constraint, is the same thing with chance; which is universally allowed to have no existence.

PART II

There is no method of reasoning more common, and yet none more blameable, than, in philosophical disputes, to endeavour the refutation of any hypothesis, by a pretence of its dangerous consequences to religion and morality. When any opinion leads to absurdities, it is certainly false; but it is not certain that an opinion is false because it is of dangerous consequence. Such topics, therefore, ought entirely to be forborne; as serving nothing to the discovery of truth, but only to make the person of an antagonist odious. This I observe in general, without pretending to draw any advantage from it. I frankly submit to an examination of this kind, and shall venture to affirm that the doctrines, both of necessity and of liberty, as above explained, are not only consistent with morality, but are absolutely essential to its support.

Necessity may be defined two ways, comformably to the two definitions of *cause*, of which it makes an essential part. It consists either in the constant conjunction of like objects, or in the inference of

---

[2] Thus, if a cause be defined, *that which produces any thing;* it is easy to observe, that *producing* is synonymous to *causing*. In like manner, if a cause be defined, *that by which any thing exists;* this is liable to the same objection. For what is meant by these words, *by which?* Had it been said, that a cause is *that* after which *any thing constantly exists;* we should have understood the terms. For this is, indeed, all we know of matter. And this constancy forms the very essence of necessity, nor have we any other idea of it.

the understanding from one object to another. Now necessity, in both these senses (which, indeed, are at bottom the same) has universally, though tacitly, in the schools, in the pulpit, and in common life, been allowed to belong to the will of man; and no one has ever pretended to deny that we can draw inferences concerning human actions, and that those inferences are founded on the experienced union of like actions, with like motives, inclinations, and circumstances. The only particular in which any one can differ, is, that either, perhaps, he will refuse to give the name of necessity to this property of human actions: But as long as the meaning is understood, I hope the word can do no harm: Or that he will maintain it possible to discover something farther in the operations of matter. But this, it must be acknowledged, can be of no consequence to morality or religion, whatever it may be to natural philosophy or metaphysics. We may here be mistaken in asserting that there is no idea of any other necessity or connexion in the actions of body: But surely we ascribe nothing to the actions of the mind, but what everyone does, and must readily allow of. We change no circumstance in the received orthodox system with regard to the will, but only in that with regard to material objects and causes. Nothing, therefore, can be more innocent, at least, than this doctrine.

All laws being founded on rewards and punishments, it is supposed as a fundamental principle, that these motives have a regular and uniform influence on the mind, and both produce the good and prevent the evil actions. We may give to this influence what name we please; but, as it is usually conjoined with the action, it must be esteemed a *cause*, and be looked upon as an instance of that necessity, which we would here establish.

The only proper object of hatred or vengeance is a person or creature, endowed with thought and consciousness; and when any criminal or injurious actions excite that passion, it is only by their relation to the person, or connexion with him. Actions are, by their very nature, temporary and perishing; and where they proceed not from some *cause* in the character and disposition of the person who performed them, they can neither redound to his honour, if good; nor infamy, if evil. The actions themselves may be blameable; they may be contrary to all the rules of morality and religion: But the person is not answerable for them; and as they proceeded from nothing in him that is durable and constant, and leave nothing of that nature behind them, it is impossible he can, upon their account, become the object of punishment or vengeance. According to the principle, therefore, which denies necessity, and consequently causes, a man is as pure and untainted, after having committed the most horrid crime, as at the first moment of his birth, nor is his character anywise concerned in his actions, since they are not derived from it, and the wickedness of the one can never be used as a proof of the depravity of the other.

Men are not blamed for such actions as they perform ignorantly and casually, whatever may be the consequences. Why? but because the principles of these actions are only momentary, and terminate in them alone. Men are less blamed for such actions as they perform hastily and unpremeditately than for such as proceed from deliberation. For what reason? but because a hasty temper, though a constant cause or principle in the mind, operates only by intervals, and infects not the whole character. Again, repentance wipes off every crime, if attended with a reformation of life and manners. How is this to be accounted for? but by asserting that actions render a person criminal merely as they are proofs of criminal principles in the mind; and when, by an alteration of these principles, they cease to be just proofs, they likewise cease to be criminal. But, except upon the doctrine of necessity, they never were just proofs, and consequently never were criminal.

It will be equally easy to prove, and from the same arguments, that *liberty,* according to that definition above mentioned, in which all men agree, is also essential to morality, and that no human actions, where it is wanting, are susceptible of any moral qualities, or can be the objects either of approbation or dislike. For as actions are objects of our moral sentiment, so far only as they are indications of the internal character, passions, and affections; it is impossible that they can give rise either to praise or blame, where they proceed not from these principles, but are derived altogether from external violence.

I pretend not to have obviated or removed all objections to this theory, with regard to necessity and liberty. I can foresee other objections, derived from topics which have not here been treated of. It may be said, for instance, that, if voluntary actions be subjected to the same laws of necessity with the operations of matter, there is a continued chain of necessary causes, preordained and predetermined, reaching from the original cause of all to every single volition of every human creature. No contingency anywhere in the universe; no indifference; no liberty. While we act, we are, at the same time, acted upon. The ultimate Author of all our volitions is the Creator of the world, who first bestowed motion on this immense machine, and placed all beings in that particular position, whence every subsequent event, by an inevitable necessity, must result. Human actions, therefore, either can have no moral turpitude at all, as proceeding from so good a cause; or if they have any turpitude, they must involve our Creator in the same guilt, while he is acknowledged to be their ultimate cause and author. For as a man who fired a mine is answerable for all the consequences whether the train he employed be long or short; so wherever a continued chain of necessary causes is fixed, that Being, either finite or infinite, who produces the first, is likewise the author of all the rest, and must both bear the blame and acquire the praise which belong to them. Our clear and unalterable ideas of morality establish this rule, upon unquestionable reasons, when we examine the consequences of any human action; and these reasons must still have greater force when applied to the volitions and intentions of a Being infinitely wise and powerful. Ignorance or impotence may be pleaded for so limited a creature as man; but those imperfections have no place in our Creator. He foresaw, he ordained, he intended all those actions of men, which we so rashly pronounce criminal. And we must therefore conclude, either that they are not criminal, or that the Deity, not man, is accountable for them. But as either of these positions is absurd and impious, it follows, that the doctrine from which they are deduced cannot possibly be true, as being liable to all the same objections. An absurd consequence, if necessary, proves the original doctrine to be absurd; in the same manner as criminal actions render criminal the original cause, if the connexion between them be necessary and evitable.

This objection consists of two parts, which we shall examine separately; *First,* that, if human actions can be traced up, by a necessary chain, to the Deity, they can never be criminal; on account of the infinite perfection of that Being from whom they are derived, and who can intend nothing but what is altogether good and laudable. Or, *Secondly,* if they be criminal, we must retract the attribute of perfection, which we ascribe to the Deity, and must acknowledge him to be the ultimate author of guilt and moral turpitude in all his creatures.

The answer to the first objection seems obvious and convincing. There are many philosophers who, after an exact scrutiny of all the phenomena of nature, conclude, that the *whole,* considered as one system, is, in every period of its existence, ordered with perfect benevolence; and that the utmost possible happiness will, in the end, result to all created beings, without any mixture of positive or absolute ill or misery. Every physical ill, say they, makes an essential part of this benevolent system, and could not possibly be removed, even by the Deity himself, considered as a wise agent, without giving entrance to greater ill, or excluding greater good, which will result from it. From this theory, some philosophers, and the ancient *Stoics* among the rest, derived a topic of consolation under all afflictions, while they taught their pupils that those ills under which they laboured were, in reality, goods to the universe; and that to an enlarged view, which could comprehend the whole system of nature, every event became an object of joy and exultation. But though this topic be specious and sublime, it was soon found in practice weak and ineffectual. You would surely more irritate than appease a man lying under the racking pains of the gout by preaching up to him the rectitude of those general laws which produced the malignant humours in his body, and led them through the proper canals, to the sinews and nerves, where they now excite such acute torments. These enlarged views may, for a moment, please the imagination of a speculative man who is placed in ease and security; but neither can they dwell with constancy on his mind, even though undisturbed by the emotions of pain or passion; much less can they maintain their ground when attacked by such powerful antagonists. The affections take a narrower and more natural survey of their object; and by an economy, more suitable to the infirmity of human minds, regard alone the beings around us, and are actuated by such events as appear good or ill to the private system.

The case is the same with *moral* as with *physical* ill. It cannot reasonably be supposed, that those remote considerations, which are found of so little efficacy with regard to one, will have a more powerful influence with regard to the other. The mind of man is so formed by nature that, upon the appearance of certain characters, dispositions, and actions, it immediately feels the sentiment of approbation or blame; nor are there any emotions more essential to its frame and constitution. The characters which engage our approbation are chiefly such as contribute to the peace and security of human society; as the characters which excite blame are chiefly such as tend to public detriment and disturbance: Whence it may reasonably be presumed, that the moral sentiments arise, either mediately or immediately, from a reflection of these opposite interests. What though philosophical meditations establish a different opinion or conjecture; that everything is right with regard to the *whole,* and that the qualities which disturb society, are, in the main, as beneficial, and are as suitable to the primary intention of nature as those which more directly promote its happiness and welfare? Are such remote and uncertain speculations able to counterbalance the sentiments which arise from the natural and immediate view of the objects? A man who is robbed of a considerable sum; does he find his vexation for the loss anywise diminished by these sublime reflections? Why then should his moral resentment against the crime be supposed incompatible with them? Or why should not the acknowledgment of a real distinction between vice and virtue be reconcileable to all speculative systems of philosophy, as well as that of a real distinction between personal beauty and deformity? Both these distinctions are founded in the natural sentiments of the human mind: And these sentiments are not to be controlled or altered by any philosophical theory or speculation whatsoever.

The *second* objection admits not of so easy and satisfactory an answer; nor is it possible to explain distinctly, how the Deity can be the mediate cause of all the actions of men, without being the author of sin and moral turpitude. These are mysteries, which mere natural and unassisted reason is very unfit to handle; and whatever system she embraces, she must find herself involved in inextricable difficulties, and even contradictions, at every step which she takes with regard to such subjects. To reconcile the indifference and contingency of human actions with prescience; or to defend absolute decrees, and yet free the Deity from being the author of sin, has been found hitherto to exceed all the power of philosophy. Happy, if she be thence sensible of her temerity, when she pries into these sublime mysteries; and leaving a scene so full of obscurities and perplexities, return, with suitable modesty, to her true and proper province, the examination of common life; where she will find difficulties enough to employ her enquiries, without launching into so boundless an ocean of doubt, uncertainty, and contradiction!

C. S. PEIRCE

The Doctrine
of Necessity Examined

I propose here to examine the common belief that every single fact in the universe is precisely determined by law. It must not be supposed that this is a doctrine accepted everywhere and at all times by all rational men. Its first advocate appears to have been Democritus, the atomist, who was led to it, as we are informed, by reflecting upon the "impenetrability, translation, and impact of matter (ἀντιτυπία καὶ φορὰ καὶ πληγὴ τῆς ὕλης)." That is to say, having restricted his attention to a field where no influence other than mechanical constraint could possibly come before his notice, he straightway jumped to the conclusion that throughout the universe that was the sole principle of action—a style of reasoning so usual in our day with men not unreflecting as to be more than excusable in the infancy of thought. But Epicurus, in revising the atomic doctrine and repairing its defences, found himself obliged to suppose that atoms swerve from their courses by spontaneous chance; and thereby he conferred upon the theory life and entelechy. For we now see clearly that the peculiar function of the molecular hypothesis in physics is to open an entry for the calculus of probabilities. Already, the prince of philosophers had repeatedly and emphatically condemned the dictum of Democritus (especially in the *Physics,* Book II, Chaps. 4, 5, 6), holding that events come to pass in three ways, namely, (1) by external compulsion, or the action of efficient

* From C. S. Peirce, "The Doctrine of Necessity Examined," *The Monist* (1892).

causes, (2) by virtue of an inward nature, or the influence of final causes, and (3) irregularly without definite cause, but just by absolute chance; and this doctrine is of the inmost essence of Aristotelianism. It affords, at any rate, a valuable enumeration of the possible ways in which anything can be supposed to have come about. The freedom of the will, too, was admitted both by Aristotle and by Epicurus. But the Stoa, which in every department seized upon the most tangible, hard, and lifeless element, and blindly denied the existence of every other, which, for example, impugned the validity of the inductive method and wished to fill its place with the *reductio ad absurdum*, very naturally became the one school of ancient philosophy to stand by a strict necessitarianism, thus returning to a single principle of Democritus that Epicurus had been unable to swallow. Necessitarianism and materialism with the Stoics went hand in hand, as by affinity they should. At the revival of learning, Stoicism met with considerable favour, partly because it departed just enough from Aristotle to give it the spice of novelty, and partly because its superficialities well adapted it for acceptance by students of literature and art who wanted their philosophy drawn mild. Afterwards, the great discoveries in mechanics inspired the hope that mechanical principles might suffice to explain the universe; and, though without logical justification, this hope has since been continually stimulated by subsequent advances in physics. Nevertheless, the doctrine was in too evident conflict with the freedom of the will and with miracles to be generally acceptable, at first. But meantime there arose that most widely spread of philosophical blunders, the notion that associationalism belongs intrinsically to the materialistic family of doctrines; and thus was evolved the theory of motives; and libertarianism became weakened. At present, historical criticism has almost exploded the miracles, great and small; so that the doctrine of necessity has never been in so great vogue as now.

The proposition in question is that the state of things existing at any time, together with certain immutable laws, completely determine the state of things at every other time (for a limitation to *future* time is indefensible). Thus, given the state of the universe in the original nebula, and given the laws of mechanics, a sufficiently powerful mind could deduce from these data the precise form of every curlicue of every letter I am now writing.

Whoever holds that every act of the will as well as every idea of the mind is under the rigid governance of a necessity coordinated with that of the physical world will logically be carried to the proposition that minds are part of the physical world in such a sense that the laws of mechanics determine anything that happens according to immutable attractions and repulsions. In that case, that instantaneous state of things, from which every other state of things is calculable, consists in the positions and velocities of all the particles at any instant. This, the usual and most logical form of necessitarianism, is called the mechanical philosophy.

When I have asked thinking men what reason they had to believe that every fact in the universe is precisely determined by law, the first answer has usually been that the proposition is a "presupposition" or postulate of scientific reasoning. Well, if that is the best that can be said for it, the belief is doomed. Suppose it be "postulated": that does not make it true, nor so much as afford the slightest rational motive for yielding it any credence. It is as if a man should come to borrow money and, when asked for his security, should reply he "postulated" the loan. To "postulate" a proposition is no more than to hope it is true. There are, indeed, practical emergencies in which we act upon assumptions of certain propositions as true, because if they are not so, it can make no difference how we act. But all such propositions I take to be hypotheses of individual facts. For it is manifest that no universal principle can in its universality be comprised in a special case or can be requisite for the validity of any ordinary inference. To say, for instance, that the demonstration by Archimedes of the property of the lever would fall to the ground if men were endowed with free will is extravagant; yet this is implied by those who make a proposition incompatible with the freedom of the will the postulate of all inference. Considering, too, that the conclusions of science make no pretense to being more than probable, and considering that a probable inference can at most only suppose something to be most frequently, or otherwise approximately, true, but never that anything is precisely true without exception throughout the universe, we see how far this proposition in truth is from being so postulated.

But the whole notion of a postulate being involved in reasoning appertains to a bygone and false conception of logic. Nondeductive or ampliative inference is of three kinds: induction, hypothesis, and analogy. If there be any other modes, they must be extremely unusual and highly complicated, and may be assumed with little doubt to be of the same nature as those enumerated. For induction, hypothesis, and analogy, as far as their ampliative character goes, that is, so far as they conclude something not implied in the premises, depend upon one principle and involve the same procedure. All are essentially inferences from sampling. Suppose a ship arrives at Liverpool laden with wheat in bulk. Suppose that by some machinery the whole cargo be stirred up with great thoroughness. Suppose that twenty-seven thimblefuls be taken equally from the forward, midships, and aft parts, from the starboard, centre, and larboard parts, and from the top, half depth, and lower parts of her hold, and that these being mixed and the grains counted, four-fifths of the latter are found to be of quality A. Then we infer, experientially and provisionally, that approximately four-fifths of all the grain in the cargo is of the same quality. I say we infer this *experientially* and *provisionally*. By saying that we infer it *experientially*, I mean that our conclusion makes no pretension to knowledge of wheat-in-itself, our ἀλήθεια, as the derivation of that word implies, has nothing to do with *latent* wheat. We are dealing only with the matter of possible experience—experience in the full acceptation of the term as something not merely affecting the senses but also as the subject of thought. If there be any wheat hidden on the ship, so that it can neither turn up in the sample nor be heard of subsequently from purchasers—or if it be half-hidden, so that it may, indeed, turn up, but is less likely to do so than the rest—or if it can affect our senses and our pockets, but from some strange cause or causelessness cannot be reasoned about—all such wheat is to be excluded (or have only its proportional weight) in calculating that true proportion of quality A, to which our inference seeks to approximate. By saying that we draw the inference *provisionally*, I mean that we do not hold that we have reached any assigned degree of approximation as yet, but only hold that if our experience be indefinitely extended, and if every fact of whatever nature, as fast as it presents itself, be duly applied, according to the inductive method, in correcting the inferred ratio, then our approximation will become indefinitely close in the long run; that is to say, close to the experience *to come* (not merely close by the exhaustion of a finite collection) so that if experience in general is to fluctuate irregularly to and fro, in a manner to deprive the ratio sought of all definite value, we shall be able to find out approximately within what limits it fluctuates; and if, after having one definite value, it changes and assumes another, we shall be able to find that out, and in short, whatever may be the variations of this ratio in experience, experience indefinitely extended will enable us to detect them, so as to predict rightly, at last, what its ultimate value may be, if it have any ultimate value, or what the ultimate law of succession of values may be, if there be any such ultimate law, or that it ultimately fluctuates irregularly within certain limits, if it do so ultimately fluctuate. Now our inference, claiming to be no more than thus experiential and provisional, manifestly involves no postulate whatever.

For what is a postulate? It is the formulation of a material fact which we are not entitled to assume as a premiss, but the truth of which is requisite to the validity of an inference. Any fact, then, which might be supposed postulated, must either be such that it would ultimately present itself in experience, or not. If it will present itself, we need not postulate it now in our provisional inference, since we shall ultimately be entitled to use it as a premiss. But if it never would present itself in experience, our conclusion is valid but for the possibility of this fact being otherwise than assumed, that is, it is valid as far as possible experience goes, and that is all that we claim. Thus, every postulate is cut off, either by the provisionality or by the experientiality of our inference. For instance, it has been said that induction postulates that, if an indefinite succession of samples be drawn, examined, and thrown back each before the next is drawn, then in the long run every grain will be drawn as often as any other, that is to say, postulates that the ratio of the numbers of times in which any two are drawn will indefinitely approximate to unity. But no such postulate is made; for if, on the one hand, we are to have no other experience of the wheat than from such drawings, it is the ratio that presents itself in those drawings and not the ratio which belongs to the wheat in its latent existence that we are endeavouring to determine; while if, on the other hand, there is some other mode by which the wheat is to come under our knowledge, equivalent to another kind of sampling, so that after all our care in stirring up the wheat some experiential grains will present themselves in the first sampling operation more often than others in the long run, this very singular fact will be sure to get discovered by the inductive method, which must avail itself of every sort of experience; and our inference, which was only provisional, corrects itself at last. Again, it has been said, that induction postulates that under like circumstances like events will happen, and that this postulate is at bottom the same as the principle of universal causation. But this is a blunder, or *bévue,* due to thinking exclusively of inductions where the concluded ratio is either 1 or 0. If any such proposition were postulated, it would be that under like circumstances (the circumstances of drawing the different samples) different events occur in the same proportions in all the different sets—a proposition which is false and even absurd. But in truth no such thing is postulated, the experiential character of the inference reducing the condition of validity to this, that if a certain result does not occur, the opposite result will be manifested, a condition assured by the provisionality of the inference. But it may be asked whether it is not conceivable that every instance of a certain class destined to be ever employed as a datum of induction should have one character, while every instance destined not to be so employed should have the opposite character. The answer is that, in that case, the instances excluded from being subjects of reasoning would not be experienced in the full sense of the word, but would be among these *latent* individuals of which our conclusion does not pretend to speak.

To this account of the rationale of induction I know of but one objection worth mention: it is that I thus fail to deduce the full degree of force which this mode of inference in fact possesses; that according to my view, no matter how thorough and elaborate the stirring and mixing process had been, the examination of a single handful of grain would not give me any assurance, sufficient to risk money upon, that the next handful would not greatly modify the concluded value of the ratio under inquiry, while, in fact, the assurance would be very high that this ratio was not greatly in error. If the true ratio of grains of quality A were 0–80 and the handful contained a thousand grains, nine such handfuls out of every ten would contain from 780 to 820 grains of quality *A*. The answer to this is that the calculation given is correct when we know that the units of this handful and the quality inquired into have the normal independence of one another, if for instance the stirring has been complete and the character sampled for has been settled upon in advance of the examination of the sample. But in so far as these conditions are not known to be complied with, the above figures cease to be applicable. Random sampling and predesignation of the character sampled for should always be striven after in inductive reasoning, but when they cannot be attained, so long as it is conducted honestly, the inference retains some value. When we cannot ascertain how the sampling has been done or the sample-character selected, induction still has the essential validity which my present account of it shows it to have.

I do not think a man who combines a willingness to be convinced with a power of appreciating an argument upon a difficult subject can resist the reasons which have been given to show that the principle of universal necessity cannot be defended as being a postulate of reasoning. But then the question immediately arises whether it is not proved to be true, or at least rendered highly probable, by observation of nature.

Still, this question ought not long to arrest a person accustomed to reflect upon the force of scientific reasoning. For the essence of the necessitarian position is that certain continuous quantities have certain exact values. Now, how can observation determine the value of such a quantity with a probable error absolutely *nil?* To one who is behind the scenes, and knows that the most refined comparisons of masses, lengths, and angles, far surpassing in precision all other measurements, yet fall behind the accuracy of bank accounts, and that the ordinary determinations of physical constants, such as appear from month to month in the journals, are about on a par with an upholsterer's measurements of carpets and curtains, the idea of mathematical exactitude being demonstrated in the laboratory will appear simply ridiculous. There is a recognized method of estimating the probable magnitudes of errors in physics—the method of least squares. It is universally admitted that this method makes the errors smaller than they really are; yet even according to that theory an error indefinitely small is indefinitely improbable; so that any statement to the effect that a certain continuous quantity has a certain exact value, if well founded at all, must be founded on something other than observation.

Still, I am obliged to admit that this rule is subject to a certain qualification. Namely, it only applies to continuous quantity. Now, certain kinds of continuous quantity are discontinuous at one or at two limits, and for such limits the rule must be modified. Thus, the length of a line cannot be less than zero. Suppose, then, the question arises how long a line a certain person had drawn from a marked point on a piece of paper. If no line at all can be seen, the observed length is zero; and the only conclusion this observation warrants is that the length of the line is less than the smallest length visible with the optical power employed. But indirect observations—for example, that the person supposed to have drawn the line was never within fifty feet of the paper—may make it probable that no line at all was made, so that the concluded length will be strictly zero. In like manner, experience no doubt would warrant the conclusion that there is absolutely *no* indigo in a given ear of wheat, and absolutely *no* attar in a given lichen. But such inferences can only be rendered valid by positive experiential evidence, direct or remote, and cannot rest upon a mere inability to detect the quantity in question. We have reason to think there is no indigo in the wheat, because we have remarked that wherever indigo is produced it is produced in considerable quantities, to mention only one argument. We have reason to think there is no attar in the lichen, because essential oils seem to be in general peculiar to single species. If the question had been whether there was iron in the wheat or the lichen, though chemical analysis should fail to detect its presence, we should think some of it probably was there, since iron is almost everywhere. Without any such information, one way or the other, we could only abstain from any opinion as to the presence of the substance in question. It cannot, I conceive, be maintained that we are in any *better* position than this in regard to the presence of the element of chance or spontaneous departures from law in nature.

Those observations which are generally adduced in favour of mechanical causation simply prove that there is an element of regularity in nature, and have no bearing whatever upon the question of whether such regularity is exact and universal or not. Nay, in regard to this *exactitude,* all observation is directly *opposed* to it; and the most that can be said is that a good deal of this observation can be explained away. Try to verify any law of nature, and you will find that the more precise your observations, the more certain they will be to show irregular departures from the law. We are accustomed to ascribe these, and I do not say wrongly, to errors of observation; yet we cannot usually account for such errors in any antecedently probable way. Trace their causes back far enough and you will be forced to admit they are always due to arbitrary determination, or chance.

But it may be asked whether if there were an element of real chance in the universe it must not occasionally be productive of signal effects such as could not pass unobserved. In answer to this question, without stopping to point out that there is an abundance of great events which one might be tempted to suppose were of that nature, it will be simplest to remark that physicists hold that the particles of gases are moving about irregularly, substantially as if by real chance, and that by the principles of probabilities there must occasionally happen to be concentrations of heat in the gases contrary to the second law of thermodynamics, and these concentrations, occurring in explosive mixtures, must sometimes have tremendous effects. Here, then, is in substance the very situation supposed; yet no phenomena ever have resulted which we are forced to attribute to such chance concentration of heat, or which anybody, wise or foolish, has ever dreamed of accounting for in that manner.

In view of all these considerations, I do not believe that anybody, not in a state of case-hardened ignorance respecting the logic of science, can maintain that the precise and universal conformity of facts to law is clearly proved, or even rendered particularly probable, by any observations hitherto made. In this way, the determined advocate of exact regularity will soon find himself driven to *a priori* reasons to support his thesis. These received such a sockdolager from Stuart Mill in his examination of Hamilton, that holding to them now seems to me to denote a high degree of imperviousness to reason, so that I shall pass them by with little notice.

To say that we cannot help believing a given proposition is no argument, but it is a conclusive fact if it be true; and with the substitution of "I" for "we," it is true in the mouths of several classes of minds: the blindly passionate, the unreflecting and ignorant, and the person who has overwhelming evidence before his eyes. But that which has been inconceivable today has often turned out indisputable on the morrow. Inability to conceive is only a stage through which every man must pass in regard to a number of beliefs—unless endowed with extraordinary obstinacy and obtuseness. His understanding is enslaved to some blind compulsion which a vigorous mind is pretty sure soon to cast off.

Some seek to back up the *a priori* position with empirical arguments. They say that the exact regularity of the world is a natural belief, and that natural beliefs have generally been confirmed by experience. There is some reason in this. Natural beliefs, however, if they generally have a foundation of truth, also require correction and purification from natural illusions. The principles of mechanics are undoubtedly natural beliefs; but, for all that, the early formulations of them were exceedingly erroneous. The general approximation to truth in natural beliefs is, in fact, a case of the general adaptation of genetic products to recognizable utilities or ends. Now, the adaptations of nature, beautiful and often marvellous as they verily are, are never found to be quite perfect; so that the argument is quite *against* the absolute exactitude of any natural belief, including that of the principle of causation.

Another argument, or convenient commonplace, is that absolute chance is *inconceivable*. This word has eight current significations. The *Century Dictionary* enumerates six. Those who talk like this will hardly be persuaded to say in what sense they mean that chance is inconceivable. Should they do so, it would easily be shown either that they have no sufficient reason for the statement or that the inconceivability is of a kind which does not prove that chance is nonexistent.

Another *a priori* argument is that chance is unintelligible; that is to say, while it may perhaps be conceivable, it does not disclose to the eye of reason the how or why of things; and since a hypothesis can only be justified so far as it renders some phenomenon intelligible, we never can have any right to suppose absolute chance to enter into the production of anything in nature. This argument may be considered in connection with two others. Namely, instead of going so far as to say that the supposition of chance can *never* properly be used to explain any observed fact, it may be alleged merely that no facts are known which such a supposition could in any way help in explaining. Or again, the allegation being still further weakened, it may be said that since departures from law are not unmistakably observed, chance is not a *vera causa,* and ought not unnecessarily to be introduced into a hypothesis.

These are no mean arguments, and require us to examine the matter a little more closely. Come, my superior opponent, let me learn from your wisdom. It seems to me that every throw of sixes with a pair of dice is a manifest instance of chance.

"While you would hold a throw of a deuce-ace to be brought about by necessity?" (The opponent's supposed remarks are placed in quotation marks.)

Clearly one throw is as much chance as another.

"Do you think throws of dice are of a different nature from other events?"

I see that I must say that *all* the diversity and specificalness of events is attributable to chance.

"Would you, then, deny that there is any regularity in the world?"

That is clearly undeniable. I must acknowledge there is an approximate regularity, and that every event is influenced by it. But the diversification, specificalness, and irregularity of things I suppose is chance. A throw of sixes appears to me a case in which this element is particularly obtrusive.

"If you reflect more deeply, you will come to see that *chance* is only a name for a cause that is unknown to us."

Do you mean that we have no idea whatever what kind of causes could bring about a throw of sixes?

"On the contrary, each die moves under the influence of precise mechanical laws."

But it appears to me that it is not these *laws* which made the die turn up sixes; for these laws act just the same when other throws come up. The chance lies in the diversity of throws; and the diversity cannot be due to laws which are immutable.

"The diversity is due to the diverse circumstances under which the laws act. The dice lie differently in the box, and the motion given to the box is different. These are the unknown causes which produce the throws, and to which we give the name of chance; not the mechanical law which regulates the operation of these causes. You see you are already beginning to think more clearly about this subject."

Does the operation of mechanical law not increase the diversity?

"Properly not. You must know that the instantaneous state of a system of particles is defined by six times as many numbers as there are particles, three for the coordinates of each particle's position, and three more for the components of its velocity. This number of numbers, which expresses the amount of diversity in the system, remains the same at all times. There may be, to be sure, some kind of relation between the coordinates and component velocities of the different particles, by means of which the state of the system might be expressed by a smaller number of numbers. But, if this is the case, a precisely corresponding relationship must exist between the coordinates and component velocities at any other time, though it may doubtless be a relation less obvious to us. Thus, the intrinsic complexity of the system is the same at all times."

Very well, my obliging opponent, we have now reached an issue. You think all the arbitrary specifications of the universe were introduced in one dose, in the beginning, if there was a beginning, and that the variety and complication of nature has always been just as much as it is now. But I, for my part, think that the diversification, the specification, has been continually taking place. Should you condescend to ask me why I so think, I should give my reasons as follows:

(1) Question any science which deals with the course of time. Consider the life of an individual animal or plant, or of a mind. Glance at the history of states, of institutions, of language, of ideas. Examine the successions of forms shown by paleontology, the history of the globe as set forth in geology, of what the astronomer is able to make out concerning the changes of stellar systems. Everywhere the main fact is growth and increasing complexity. Death and corruption are mere accidents or secondary phenomena. Among some of the lower organisms, it is a moot point with biologists whether there be anything which ought to be called death. Races, at any rate, do not die out except under unfavourable circumstances. From these broad and ubiquitous facts we may fairly infer, by the most unexceptionable logic, that there is probably in nature some agency by which the complexity and diversity of things can be increased; and that conse-

quently the rule of mechanical necessity meets in some way with interference.

(2) By thus admitting pure spontaneity or life as a character of the universe, acting always and everywhere though restrained within narrow bounds by law, producing infinitesimal departures from law continually, and great ones with infinite infrequency, I account for all the variety and diversity of the universe, in the only sense in which the really *sui generis* and new can be said to be accounted for. The ordinary view has to admit the inexhaustible multitudinous variety of the world, has to admit that its mechanical law cannot account for this in the least, that variety can spring only from spontaneity, and yet denies without any evidence or reason the existence of this spontaneity, or else shoves it back to the beginning of time and supposes it dead ever since. The superior logic of my view appears to me not easily controverted.

(3) When I ask the necessitarian how he would explain the diversity and irregularity of the universe, he replies to me out of the treasury of his wisdom that irregularity is something which from the nature of things we must not seek to explain. Abashed at this, I seek to cover my confusion by asking how he would explain the uniformity and regularity of the universe, whereupon he tells me that the laws of nature are immutable and ultimate facts, and no account is to be given of them. But my hypothesis of spontaneity does explain irregularity, in a certain sense; that is, it explains the general fact of irregularity, though not, of course, what each lawless event is to be. At the same time, by thus loosening the bond of necessity, it gives room for the influence of another kind of causation, such as seems to be operative in the mind in the formation of associations, and enables us to understand how the uniformity of nature could have been brought about. That single events should be hard and unintelligible, logic will permit without difficulty: we do not expect to make the shock of a personally experienced earthquake appear natural and reasonable by any amount of cogitation. But logic does expect things *general* to be understandable. To say that there is a universal law, and that it is a hard, ultimate, unintelligible fact, the why and wherefore of which can never be inquired into, at this a sound logic will revolt, and will pass over at once to a method of philosophizing which does not thus barricade the road of discovery.

(4) Necessitarianism cannot logically stop short of making the whole action of the mind a part of the physical universe. Our notion that we decide what we are going to do, if, as the necessitarian says, it has been calculable since the earliest times, is reduced to illusion. Indeed, consciousness in general thus becomes a mere illusory aspect of a material system. What we call red, green, and violet are in reality only different rates of vibration. The sole reality is the distribution of qualities of matter in space and time. Brain-matter is protoplasm in a certain degree and kind of complication—a certain arrangement of mechanical particles. Its feeling is but an inward aspect, a phantom. For, from the positions and velocities of the particles at any one instant, and the knowledge of the immutable forces, the positions at all other times are calculable; so that the universe of space, time, and matter is a rounded system uninterfered with from elsewhere. But, from the state of feeling at any instant, there is no reason to suppose the states of feeling at all other instants are thus exactly calculable; so that feeling is, as I said, a mere fragmentary and illusive aspect of the universe. This is the way, then, that necessitarianism has to make up its accounts. It enters consciousness under the head of sundries, as a forgotten trifle; its scheme of the universe would be more satisfactory if this little fact could be dropped out of sight. On the other hand, by supposing the rigid exactitude of causation to yield, I care not how little—be it but by a strictly infinitesimal amount—we gain room to insert mind into our scheme, and to put it into the place where it is needed, into the position which, as the sole self-intelligible thing, it is entitled to occupy, that of the fountain of existence; and in so doing we resolve the problem of the connection of soul and body.

(5) But I must leave undeveloped the chief of my reasons, and can only adumbrate it. The hypothesis of chance-spontaneity is one whose inevitable consequences are capable of being traced out with mathematical precision into considerable detail. Much of this I have done and find the consequences to agree with observed facts to an extent which seems to me remarkable. But the matter and methods of reasoning are novel, and I have no right to promise that other mathematicians shall find my deductions as satisfactory as I myself do, so that the strongest reason for my belief must for the present remain a private reason of my own, and cannot influence others. I

mention it to explain my own position; and partly to indicate to future mathematical speculators a veritable gold mine, should time and circumstances and the abridger of all joys prevent my opening it to the world.

If now I, in my turn, inquire of the necessitarian why he prefers to suppose that all specification goes back to the beginning of things, he will answer me with one of those last three arguments which I left unanswered.

First, he may say that chance is a thing absolutely unintelligible, and therefore that we never can be entitled to make such a supposition. But does not this objection smack of naïve impudence? It is not mine, it is his own conception of the universe which leads abruptly up to hard, ultimate, inexplicable, immutable law, on the one hand, and to inexplicable specification and diversification of circumstances on the other. My view, on the contrary, hypothesizes nothing at all, unless it be hypothesis to say that all specification came about in some sense, and it is not to be accepted as unaccountable. To undertake to account for anything by saying baldly that it is due to chance would, indeed, be futile. But this I do not do. I make use of chance chiefly to make room for a principle of generalization, or tendency to form habits, which I hold has produced all regularities. The mechanical philosopher leaves the whole specification of the world utterly unaccounted for, which is pretty nearly as bad as to baldly attribute it to chance. I attribute it altogether to chance, it is true, but to chance in the form of a spontaneity which is to some degree regular. It seems to me clear at any rate that one of these two positions must be taken, or else specification must be supposed due to a spontaneity which develops itself in a certain and not in a chance way, by an objective logic like that of Hegel. This last way I leave as an open possibility, for the present; for it is as much opposed to the necessitarian scheme of existence as my own theory is.

Secondly, the necessitarian may say there are, at any rate, no observed phenomena which the hypothesis of chance could aid in explaining. In reply, I point first to the phenomenon of growth and developing complexity, which appears to be universal, and which, though it may possibly be an affair of mechanism perhaps, certainly presents all the appearance of increasing diversification. Then, there is variety itself, beyond comparison the most obtrusive character of the universe: no mechanism can account for this. Then, there is the very fact the necessitarian most insists upon, the regularity of the universe which for him serves only to block the road of inquiry. Then, there are the regular relationships between the laws of nature —similarities and comparative characters, which appeal to our intelligence as its cousins, and call upon us for a reason. Finally, there is consciousness, feeling, a patent fact enough, but a very inconvenient one to the mechanical philosopher.

Thirdly, the necessitarian may say that chance is not a *vera causa,* that we cannot know positively there is any such element in the universe. But the doctrine of the *vera causa* has nothing to do with elementary conceptions. Pushed to that extreme, it at once cuts off belief in the existence of a material universe; and without that necessitarianism could hardly maintain its ground. Besides, variety is a fact which must be admitted; and the theory of chance merely consists in supposing this diversification does not antedate all time. Moreover, the avoidance of hypotheses involving causes nowhere positively known to act is only a recommendation of logic, not a positive command. It cannot be formulated in any precise terms without at once betraying its untenable character—I mean as rigid rule, for as a recommendation it is wholesome enough.

I believe I have thus subjected to fair examination all the important reasons for adhering to the theory of universal necessity, and have shown their nullity. I earnestly beg that whoever may detect any flaw in my reasoning will point it out to me, either privately or publicly; for, if I am wrong, it much concerns me to be set right speedily. If my argument remains unrefuted, it will be time, I think, to doubt the absolute truth of the principle of universal law; and when once such a doubt has obtained a living root in any man's mind, my cause with him, I am persuaded, is gained.

ERNEST NAGEL

Determinism in History

~~~~~~

Some thirty years ago, a historian of some eminence examined the apparently decisive influence exercised by a number of famous persons upon such important historical occurrences as the Protestant Reformation in England, the American Revolution, and the development of parliamentary government. He then assessed the supposedly critical role which the decisions and actions of these men played in bringing about those events, generalized his findings, and concluded as follows:

> These great changes seem to have come about with a certain inevitableness; there seems to have been an independent trend of events, some inexorable necessity controlling the progress of human affairs. . . . Examined closely, weighed and measured carefully, set in true perspective, the personal, the casual, the individual influences in history sink in significance and great cyclical forces loom up. Events come of themselves, so to speak; that is, they come so consistently and unavoidably as to rule out as causes not only physical phenomena but voluntary human action. So arises the conception of *law in history*. History, the great course of human affairs, has not been the result of voluntary efforts on the part of individuals or groups of individuals, much less chance; but has been subject to law.
>
> (Edward P. Cheney, *Law in History and Other Essays*, New York, 1927, p. 7.)

* From Ernest Nagel, "Determinism in History," *Philosophy and Phenomenological Research*, XX, No. 3 (March, 1960), 291–317. Reprinted by permission of the editor and the author.

The view expressed in this quotation is a variant of a conception of human affairs that is familiar and continues to be widely held. It is a conception that has sometimes been advanced as ancillary to a theodicy; sometimes to a romantic philosophy of cosmic organicism; sometimes to an ostensibly "scientific" theory of civilization which finds the causes of human progress or decline in the operations of impersonal factors such as geography, race, or economic organization. Despite important differences between them, these various doctrines of historical inevitability share a common premise: the impotence of deliberate human action, whether individual or concerted, to alter the course of human history, since historical changes are allegedly the products of deep-lying forces which conform to fixed, though perhaps not always known, patterns of development.

It is not my aim here to discuss this doctrine of historical inevitability. That doctrine has not lacked effective critics, and in recent years it has been subjected to severe scrutiny by numerous historians and philosophers. I would like to say in passing, however, that I agree with its critics in holding it to be untenable. In some of its variant forms the doctrine can indeed be shown to have no empirical content, since in those versions notions are employed such that no conceivable empirical evidence can ever be relevant for evaluating the doctrine as true or false. But even when it is formulated as a factually verifiable statement, the available evidence supports neither the thesis that all human events illustrate a unitary, transculturally invariant law of historical development, nor the thesis that individual or concerted human effort never operates as a decisive factor in the transformations of society. In asserting all this I am, of course, not denying that in many historical situations individual choice and effort may count for little or nothing. On the contrary, I want to affirm explicitly that frequently there are ascertainable limits to human power, whether individual or collective, for directing the course of historical changes—limits that may be set by facts of physics and geography, by biological endowment, by modes of economic production and available technological skills, by tradition and political organization, by human stupidity and ignorance, as well as by various antecedent historical occurrences.

On the other hand, many recent critics of historical inevitability have not stopped with denying the manifestly exaggerated claims of this doctrine. They have gone on to challenge what they believe is the basic assumption underlying that doctrine, an assumption to which that doctrine is supposedly but an easy corollary. More specifically, a growing number of thinkers has been claiming that what is really at the bottom of beliefs in historical inevitability is the very notion that human events generally occur only under determinate and determining conditions. Many writers have in consequence argued that a thoroughgoing determinism is incompatible with the established facts of history as well as with a genuinely significant imputation to human beings of responsibility for their choices and actions. In the eyes of many, furthermore, it is this deterministic assumption which is ultimately behind current attempts at extending behavioristic (or more generally, naturalistic) methods of inquiry into the study of human affairs; and the undeniable crudities which have sometimes accompanied the use of such methods, have been therefore cited as the unavoidable fruits of the deterministic assumption itself. Accordingly, a number of critics of historical inevitability have also trained their fire on the putative deterministic premise of much current psychological and social research; they have challenged the worth of such research in effect because of its allegedly disruptive effects on vital beliefs in human freedom and in the validity of any judgment ascribing responsibility to individual persons for any of their actions.

It would not be difficult to suggest plausible explanations, psychological and sociological, based on the events of the past few decades, for the current intellectual hostility toward the assumption of a thoroughgoing determinism in human history. It is not my aim, however, to propose such explanations. I wish, instead, to examine the major arguments as I have encountered them which have been advanced in criticism of determinism, and to indicate where they seem to be mistaken. I hope thereby to show that critics of historical inevitability who have argued for either a radical or a qualified indeterminism in human affairs, have rejected one extreme position only to adopt another one no less extreme and dubious.

I

I must, however, first state briefly what is to be understood by "determinism," and also indicate summarily what I believe to be the cognitive status of the general assumption of determinism.

There are writers, like the Dutch historian Pieter Geyl, who construe it as the doctrine "according to which we are helplessly caught in the grip of a movement proceeding from all that has gone before." (Pieter Geyl, *Debates with Historians,* New York, 1956, p. 236.) But if we adopt such a definition, and take strictly the phrase "helplessly caught" or its equivalents, we are committed from the outset not only to identifying determinism with a particular and even mistaken interpretation of historical processes. We are also committed to a formulation that makes the issue of determinism, as discussed traditionally as well as currently, of doubtful relevance to the analysis of most branches of knowledge. I think, however, that this issue is not foreign to such analyses; and it is therefore desirable to formulate the doctrine in a manner that does not preclude its pertinence to extensive areas of scientific inquiry.

Let me sketch a definition of "determinism" in terms of an example that is generally familiar, relatively simple, and commonly regarded as a deterministic one. I borrow the example from a discussion of a physiochemical system by the late physiologist, Lawrence J. Henderson. (*Pareto's General Sociology,* Cambridge, Mass., 1937, Chap. 3.) The system consists of a mixture of soda-water, whisky, and ice, contained in a sealed vacuum bottle. We assume for the sake of simplicity that no air is present in the bottle, or at any rate that if air is present it can be ignored. We also assume that the mixture is completely isolated from other systems, for example, from sources of heat in the environment, from the influence of electric and gravitational fields, and so on. It is of great importance to note, moreover, that the sole characteristics of the system which are of concern are its so-called thermodynamical ones, and that any other traits which the system may exhibit fall outside of this discussion. In particular, the factors (or "variables") to which attention is here directed include the following: the *number of components* of the system (the components here are water, alcohol, and carbon dioxide); the *phases* or types of aggregation in which the components occur (*i.e.,* whether they occur in a solid, liquid, or gaseous phase); the *concentrations* of the components in each phase; the *temperature* of the mixture; its *pressure* on the walls of the container; and so on. Now it is well known that under the stipulated conditions, and for a given temperature and pressure, each component will occur in the various phases with definite concentrations; and conversely, if the concentrations are fixed, the temperature and pressure will have a unique set of values. Thus, if the pressure of the mixture were increased (for example, by pressing down the stopper of the bottle), the concentration of water in the gaseous phase would be reduced, and its concentration in the liquid phase would be increased; and analogously for a change in temperature. It is therefore evident that the variables of the system which are under consideration stand to each in definite relations of interdependence. Accordingly, I propose to say that the value of a variable at any given time is "determined" by the values of the other variables at that time.

But we can go one step further, and indicate what is to be understood by saying that the system as a whole is a deterministic one. Suppose that at some initial time, the system is in a definite *state*— that is, the variables of the system have certain fixed values; suppose that because of a change induced in one or more of those values at that time, the system moves into another state after an interval of time t; and suppose, finally, that the system is brought back in some way to its initial state, that the same changes are induced in the variables as before, and that after the same interval of time t the system again is in the second state. If, now, the system behaves in this manner, no matter what state is taken to be the initial state and no matter what interval of time t is specified for the duration of its development into the second state, then the system will be said to be a deterministic one in respect to the indicated class of characteristics or variables. It is evident that if a deterministic system is in a definite state at a given time, the occurrence of that state at that time is determined—in the sense that the necessary and sufficient condition for the occurrence of that state at that time is that the system was in a certain state at a certain previous time. Moreover, if a variable of the system has a certain value at a given time, that value can be said to be determined by the state of the system at any prior time —that is to say, the necessary and sufficient condition for that variable of the system having that value at that time is that the system was in some definite state at some prior time.

This skeletal account of what is to be understood by a deterministic system can be generalized and made more precise. In particular, it can be extended to include systems whose characteristics are not (and perhaps cannot be) represented by numerically measurable variables. It can also be broadened so as to cover systems whose "macroscopic" or "molar" characteristics may be said to be determined by the structures and characteristics of certain "microscopic" constituents of those systems—as in the case of the thermal properties of a gas being contingent on the occurrence of certain relations between the molecules of the gas. Space is lacking, however, for presenting a more generalized and technically more adequate definition of determinism, though enough has been said to suggest how such an analysis would proceed.

But there are several points in this account to which special attention must be directed. In the first place, it is immediately clear that when determinism is understood in the above sense, the assumption that a system is deterministic does *not* entail that the states of the system are *predictable*—whether from prior states of the system or from the states of the microscopic parts of the system. Accordingly, a system may be a deterministic one, though we may not know that it is such; and it is a mistake to identify, as some influential philosophers seem to have done, the meaning of "determinism" with the possibility of prediction with unlimited accuracy. On the other hand, both our practical and theoretical interests are directed toward discovering certain regularities in the operations of various systems, with a view to formulating laws or rules that may enable us to predict (or retrodict) the occurrences of events and their characteristics. Indeed, we have been remarkably successful, in the case of many systems, in constructing theories which are instrumental to highly precise predictions of many varieties of events. Moreover, we can rarely be certain in formulating such laws that all the necessary and sufficient conditions for the occurrence of events and processes have been enumerated. Nevertheless, most of our practical interests, and even some of our theoretical ones, are satisfied if we suceed in stating only some of the necessary conditions whose own existence is relatively impermanent or sporadic, provided that "other things are equal" and provided that when those conditions do become actualized (perhaps because we are able to control their occurrence) the events in question are also realized.

In the second place, it will also be clear that, while a given system may be deterministic with respect to one set of properties, it need not necessarily be deterministic with respect to some other set. Moreover, while the occurrence of a given set of properties exhibited by one system may not be determined by a prescribed class of characteristics also exhibited by that system, the occurrence of those properties may be determined by other characteristics manifested in some other system. Accordingly, should we have reason to believe that a given system is not deterministic in respect to a specified set of properties, at least two alternatives are in principle open to us. We may have evidence to show that the system is not an isolated one; and we may therefore either make allowances for the disturbing influences which play upon it from the "outside," or enlarge the system so that it is taken to be part of a more *inclusive* deterministic system. The other alternative is to attribute the apparent indeterminism of the system to an incomplete or incorrect analysis of the system itself. We may then, for example, come to regard it as made up of a differently specified set of parts or processes, and so perhaps discover that the macroscopic states of the system are determined by certain of its microscopic states.

In the third place, determinism in its most general form appears to be the claim that for every set of characteristics which may occur at any time, there is some system that is deterministic in respect to those occurrences. Now it is easy to see that determinism so construed has not been conclusively established, nor can it be conclusively refuted by the outcome of any empirical investigation. It has not been conclusively established, since there are perhaps an endless number of classes of events for which we do not yet know the determining conditions; and it is at least logically possible that for some of those classes of events no determining conditions in fact exist. On the other hand, determinism cannot be definitively disproved, since our failure to discover the determining conditions for some event (or type of event) does not prove that there are in fact no such conditions. In my view, therefore, a doctrine of universal determinism can be defended only partly on the ground that it is a correct generalized description of the world as we actually know it; and its operative role in inquiry seems to me to be that of a guiding principle, which formulates in a comprehensive fashion one of the major objectives of positive science.

It is worth noting, however, that determinism functions most effectively as a regulative principle, when the highly generalized formulation suggested above is replaced by a more specific one—one which stipulates more or less definitely what sort of characteristics are to be looked into in our search for the determining conditions of various types of events. For example, in the Laplacian version of determinism, the determining conditions for all occurrences are taken to be the positions and momenta of mass-particles, together with certain dynamic relations (classically called "forces") between the latter. It is a familiar fact that the Laplacian notion of determinism was for a time a fruitful guiding principle for an extensive class of investigations, although its fertility eventually became exhausted, and by the end of the nineteenth century physical scientists adopted other special forms of the deterministic assumption. No comparably fruitful specializations of this assumption have been proposed in the psychological and social sciences—although in these areas of study particular forms of determinism have also led to important findings, for example, those which have directed attention to such determining factors as heredity, attitudes acquired by training, repetition of exposure to stimuli, modes of economic production or social stratification and social mobility.

Although such specializations of the deterministic assumption may have only a limited range of adequacy, enough has been said to make clear that the inadequacies of these special forms do not constitute a definite disproof of the general deterministic principle. Nor do I believe, though I cannot here advance any supporting arguments, and despite the almost unanimous opinion of contemporary physicists to the contrary, that current developments in quantum theory have established the untenability of a universal determinism as a generalized regulative principle.

These considerations, though somewhat abstract and initially remote from my theme, have a direct bearing on current objections to the use of deterministic assumptions in the study of human history. What, then, are the arguments which have led so many recent thinkers to reject such assumptions? I shall examine the main reasons that have been advanced for such rejection under the following convenient heads: (1) the argument from the non-existence of so-called "necessary laws of development" in human history; (2) the argument from the unpredictability and inexplicability of human events; (3) the argument from the emergence of novelties in human affairs; (4)

the argument from the occurrence of chance events in human history; and (5) the argument from the incompatibility of determinism with the reality of human freedom and with the attribution of moral responsibility.

II

The first argument can be quickly dismissed. It is directed primarily against those grandiose philosophies of history, whether religious or secular in orientation, which claim to find either a definite pattern of development in the apparently chaotic story of the entire human race, or at any rate a fixed order of change repeatedly exhibited by each human society or civilization. On this view, accordingly, every human act has a definite place in an unalterable or timeless structure of changes, and each society must necessarily pass through a definite series of antecedent changes before it can achieve a subsequent stage. Moreover, though human individuals are the ostensible agents which bring about the movement of history, in most of these philosophies human actions are at best only the "instruments" through which certain "forces," operating and evolving in conformity with fixed laws, become manifest.

Philosophies of history of this type often possess the fascination of great dramatic literature; and few of their readers would be willing to deny the remarkable imaginative powers and amazing erudition that frequently go into their construction. As I have already indicated, however, the historical evidence, when such evidence is at all relevant for judging such philosophies, is overwhelmingly negative; and like most of their current critics I feel safe in rejecting them as false.

But does it follow from the falsity of the doctrine of historical inevitability that there are no causal connections in history, and that determinism in history is a myth? Those recent critics of the doctrine who believe that it does follow, offer no explicit grounds for their claim, and appear to base their contention on what I think is an extraordinarily narrow conception of what a deterministic system must be like. For they appear to assume that astronomy supplies the typical example of such a system; and they tacitly suppose that since human history does not exhibit the stability and the regular periodicity of the solar system, historical events cannot possibly be elements in a deterministic system. In point of fact, however, some of the familiar features of the solar system are not representative of most deterministic systems. For the relatively unchanging periodicity of planetary motions, for example, is contingent upon the continued relative isolation of the system from the influence of other bodies in remote regions of space, as well as from the effects of various changes within the system (such as chemical or biological ones) that are formally excluded from the province of celestial mechanics—a circumstance which is rarely encountered in connection with most deterministic systems even in the natural sciences. Thus, a straw flying in the wind exhibits no such familiar regularities as do the planets, not because we have reason to believe that the motion of the straw is not determined by definite dynamic properties, but because some of these determining factors are undergoing rapid (and indeed unknown) variations. The crucial point to note is that while a given system may fail to exhibit some special pattern of regular behavior, it may nevertheless manifest a more complex, because less uniform, pattern of changes; and it also may happen that certain apparently random changes in parts of the system depend on variable factors located in other parts of the system. Accordingly, even if there are no laws of historical development, as claimed by proponents of historical inevitability, it may still be the case, for example, that the rise of the towns in tenth-century northern Europe was determined at least in part by the Mohammedan interruption of the Mediterranean trade, that the decline of Spanish power in the seventeenth century was in part the consequence of Spanish economic and colonial policy, or that a necessary condition for the entrance of the United States into the First World War was the adoption by Germany of an unrestricted submarine warfare. In short, the argument against determinism from the nonexistence of historical laws of development, does not achieve its objective.

III

Critics of determinism in history place much weight on the essential inexplicability and unpredictability of historical events. This argument is frequently coupled with a strong emphasis on the "creative novelties" which emerge from human actions and which constitute at least part of the ground for the alleged unpredictability of historical changes; but I shall postpone discussing this latter point. Even so, there are several dimensions to the present argument, and I shall consider them in turn.

(1) Let me first quickly dispose of an argument, repeatedly used by Charles Beard, to support the conclusion that historical occurrences are basically inexplicable. In substance, the argument claims that all attempts at an explanation of what happens in human history lead to an endless regress, since even if we succeed in discovering the conditions for the occurrence of an event, the occurrence of those conditions will need to be explained in terms of the occurrence of another set of antecedent conditions, and so on without limit. (Thus Beard declared: "A search for the causes of America's entry into the [First World War] leads into the causes of the war, into all the history that lies beyond 1914, and into the very nature of the universe of which history is a part; that is, unless we arbitrarily decide to cut the web and begin at some point that pleases us." *The Discussion of Human Affairs*, New York, 1936, p. 79; *cf.* also pp. 68 ff.)

Such an objection to the possibility of explanation, however, is absurd. If it were sound, no explanations for the occurrence of events could be achieved, neither in the social nor in the natural sciences. But the retort to it is obvious. Although C may be the cause or a determining condition for B, where B is a condition for the occurrence of A, B is nonetheless a determining factor for A; and in stating the determinants for B, we are answering a different question from the one we are seeking to resolve when we ask for the determinants of A. In brief, an explanation can be completely satisfactory, even though in offering it we are assuming something which has not in turn been also explained.

(2) There is another issue, largely verbal, which will also require only brief attention. It has already been mentioned that a number of recent writers have identified the meaning of "determined" as the possibility of making predictions with unlimited precision. Moreover, according to current quantum theory there are definite theoretical limits to the degree of precision with which subatomic processes can be predicted. These writers have therefore concluded that the general deterministic assumption must be judged as either false

or as inapplicable to a large class of occurrences. (*Cf.*, for example, Moritz Schlick, "Die Kausalität i.d. gegenwärtigen Physik," *Gesammelte Aufsätze*, pp. 73–74.)

Is it plausible, however, to equate except by fiat the meanings of the words "determined" and "predictable"? It is customary in this connection to distinguish two senses of "predictable" or its opposite "unpredictable." In one sense, an event is unpredictable if, because of the state of our knowledge and our technology at a given time, the event cannot be foretold at all, or only with some degree of precision. In the second sense of the word, an event is *theoretically* unpredictable if the assumption that its occurrence can be calculated in advance, either at all or with unlimited precision, is incompatible with some accepted theory of science. In neither of these senses, however, is "unpredictable" synonymous with "undetermined" (or "predictable" with "determined")—at any rate not when "determined" has the meaning I have suggested for it. For on that meaning the occurrence of solar eclipses, for example, may be determined, despite the fact that some primitive tribes lack the knowledge for anticipating them, and despite the fact that the ancient Babylonians were able to predict them with far less precision than we can. Moreover, even though quantum theory places an upper bound on the precision with which subatomic processes are predictable, it surely is not nonsense to hold, as Planck, Einstein, and De Broglie have in fact held whether correctly or mistakenly, that an alternative theory may eventually be constructed which will not impose such theoretical limits on precise predictions in that domain. Accordingly, the verbal gambit which stipulates the synonymy of "determined" and "predictable," does not dispose of the issue raised by critics of the assumption of determinism in human history.

(3) Let us turn to more substantive problems related to the predictability of human events. Are such events utterly unpredictable in fact? It would be just silly to maintain that the whole of the human future is predictable by us, or that our present information suffices for retrodicting every event in the human past. But it would also be absurd to hold that we are completely incompetent to do any of these things with reasonable assurance of being correct. It is banal to note that our personal relations with other men, our political arrangements and social institutions, our transportation

schedules, and our administration of justice, could not be what they are, unless fairly safe inferences were possible about the human past and future. As I write this line, we cannot predict with certainty who will be the next president of the United States. But if we take for granted current American attitudes toward domestic and foreign powers, and also take into account the present alignment of the world powers, we do have good grounds for confidence that there will be a presidential election this year, that neither major political party will nominate a Communist sympathizer, and that the successful candidate will be neither a woman nor a Negro. These various predictions are indefinite in certain ways, for they do not foretell the future in a manner to exclude all conceivable alternatives but one. Nevertheless, they *do* exclude an enormous number of logical possibilities for the coming year; and they do point up the fact that though the human beings who will participate in those coming events may have a considerable range of free choice in their actions, their actual choices and actions will fall within certain limits. The obvious import of all this is that not everything which is logically possible is also historically possible during a given period and for a given society of men; and the equally obvious interpretation of this fact is that there are determining conditions for both what has happened as well as what will happen in human history.

(4) It is nevertheless pertinent to ask why even our subsequent historical explanations of past human events, to say nothing of our forecasts of future ones, are almost invariably imprecise and incomplete. For our accounts of past occurrences, whether these be individual or collective acts, rarely if ever explain the exact details of what did happen, and succeed in exhibiting only the grounds which make *probable* the occurrence of a more or less vaguely (or precisely) formulated characteristic.

It will be helpful to recall the ideal logical structure of an explanation. That structure is usually described as that of a formally valid deductive argument, whose conclusion is a statement formulating the event to be explained, and whose premises contain one or more statements of universal laws (expressing some assumed invariable connections of attributes or relations), as well as relevant singular statements that specify the initial and boundary conditions for applying those laws to the case at hand.

This logical structure can be amply illustrated by examples of explanation in many areas of inquiry, especially when what is being explained is some *law* (rather than some particular *event*) on the basis of other laws or theories. But it is notorious that the explanations encountered in the study of human affairs do not conform strictly to this pattern; and it is at least a debatable question whether that pattern is fully embodied in explanations of concrete, individual occurrences even in the natural sciences—except perhaps in rare cases (as in the case of events occurring under carefully controlled laboratory conditions). The deductive structure of explanation thus appears to represent what may at best be a limiting or ideal case in historical study. I proceed to mention several reasons, most of them perhaps quite familiar, why this is so.

(a) As just noted, an explanation of a particular event ideally includes among its premises the set of initial and boundary conditions for the application of assumed universal laws; and in specifying those conditions, the explanation states the sufficient conditions for the occurrence of the event. But even if we knew all the relevant laws pertaining to the traits of an event under study, we are rarely if ever in the position in historical investigations to specify more than a fraction of the initial conditions for the application of those laws. Because of our ignorance of many if not of most of these initial data, we can therefore state only some of the *necessary* conditions for historical occurrences. For this reason alone, accordingly, explanations in history do not have the structure of a straightforward deductive argument.

Nevertheless, this circumstance hardly constitutes evidence against determinism in history; on the contrary, it testifies to the dependence of events on the occurrence of other contingencies additional to those we can usually identify. Indeed, explanations of particular happenings in the natural sciences face difficulties essentially comparable to those encountered in historical inquiry. These difficulties are often concealed even in physics, by the tacit assumption of a *ceteris paribus* clause, where the "other things" which are supposedly "constant" are frequently unknown or are only hazarded. For example, the path traversed by a bullet can be explained with the help of the Newtonian theory of mechanics and gravitation. That explanation may explicitly mention such items as the muzzle-velocity of the projectile or the resistance of the air; but it will not mention the position of the earth in relation to our own and other galactic systems. The explanation ignores this latter fact because on the theory which it employs the mass of the bullet is constant, and independent not only of the velocity of the body but also of its distances from other bodies. However, as Mach pointed out in his critique of Newtonian theory, it may well be that the inertia of a body is a function of its distance from all other bodies in the universe. This observation, baptized as "Mach's Principle," receives serious attention in current physical cosmology, though the possibility which it notes apparently was never considered prior to Mach. One important difference between explanations of particular events in the natural and social sciences thus seems to be that while in the former we frequently have no good reasons for supposing that the conditions we mention for the occurrence of an event are not sufficient, in the latter we are usually acutely aware that the conditions we cite are only necessary.

(b) There is, however, a further point about explanations in history that is perhaps even more important. In the ideal pattern of explanation, the generalizations included in the premises are assumed to be strictly universal in form. But in historical studies the generalizations we tacitly invoke are rarely if ever plausible if they are asserted with strict universality; they are credible only if they are construed as formulating statistical regularities. Moreover, the characterizations employed in those generalizations are usually vague; and if they are defined at all, in order to introduce greater precision into our account of things, they are made more definite only in some quasi-statistical manner. In consequence, in applying such generalizations to particular occurrences, there may be considerable uncertainty whether the given occurrence properly falls under those generalizations. Accordingly, and quite apart from the question whether we can specify all the requisite initial conditions for the application of assumed laws, the statement asserting the occurrence of the event to be explained does not follow *deductively* from the premises; that statement stands to the explanatory premises which we can assert with a measure of warrant, only in some relation of probability.

The point is important enough to merit an illustration. At the time of his death Henry VIII's official style read essentially as follows: By the Grace of God, King of England, Ireland and France, Defender of the Faith and Only Supreme Head of the Church of England and Ireland. But when Elizabeth succeeded to the throne in 1558, eleven years later, she proclaimed herself: By the Grace of God, Queen of England, Ireland and France, Defender of the Faith, *etc.*, and she was the first English sovereign to *etcetrate* herself in an unabbreviated official title. Why did she do so? F. W. Maitland, the legal historian, offered an explanation. He produced evidence to show that the introduction of the "etcetra" was not a slip, but was a deliberate act which sought to conceal her plans, for the time being at least, concerning the difficult Roman question. Maitland in effect argued that because the alignment of political forces both at home and abroad was unsettled, and because a clear stand by her on the future relation of the English Church to Rome was fraught with grave perils no matter how she decided, she won for herself freedom of action by employing a style in which her eventual decision on this issue was ambiguously stated.

Now an examination of Maitland's discussion shows beyond doubt that the event he sought to explain does indeed logically follow from the explanatory premises, provided these include an assumption essentially as follows: Whenever anyone acquires a position of great political power, is faced with an issue fraught with peril, but is required to announce immediately a policy, then such a person will make a statement that is momentarily noncommittal. However, such an assumption, if asserted universally, is clearly false; and it is plausible only if it is construed as holding either for the most part or in some appreciable fraction of cases. But if this emended generalization is adopted, the fact to be explained no longer follows strictly from the premises. Furthermore, even in the emended form the generalization makes use of the notion of a policy decision involving uncertain dangers; and it is clear that this notion is a vague one. Indeed, though we might conceivably agree that a policy is dangerous to a maximal degree only if it possesses a certain set of specified traits, we would ordinarily classify a policy as dangerous even if it possessed only some undetermined fraction of those traits. In subsuming the decision which Elizabeth was required to make under the heading "being fraught with peril," we are thus characterizing it in an essentially statistical fashion; and we may be therefore not at all sure that the generalization, even in its emended form, is actually applicable to the case under discussion.

(5) There is accordingly little doubt that typical explanations in history are in an obvious sense incomplete, since they specify what is at best only some of the necessary conditions for the occurrence of events. But before commenting on the import of this point for the issue of determinism, let us consider one further crucial issue: Granted that we have not succeeded in discovering strictly universal laws which would account completely for historical events, and which would indicate the sufficient conditions for their occurrence, are there reasons of principle for our failure, or are there reasons for believing that our failures may be only temporary?

An adequate answer to these questions must take into account the frequently neglected though familiar point that in providing explanations for historical events, historians usually operate on certain typical (and often conventionally set) levels of analysis—despite the possibility that causal determinants for those events may be found on various other levels of analysis. Historians are in the main habitually interested in accounting for the occurrence of only a somewhat limited class of traits; and they normally also seek to explain them in terms of a comparably restricted set of traits characterizing events. Thus Maitland was concerned with explaining the *ambiguity* occurring in Elizabeth's title; and he evidently did not set himself the task of explaining her use of the *specific* locution "etcetra," rather than some other form of ambiguity. Nor was he interested in explaining the occurrence of Elizabeth's particular facial expression or the amount of her blood pressure, which were also parts or phases of the event in which she conceived the ambiguous locution. Furthermore, Maitland explained her adoption of an ambiguous title in terms of Elizabeth's political intelligence and the alignment of politically powerful groups. It evidently did not occur to him to account for the ambiguous form of her title in terms of such factors as the details of her individual psychology or her particular physiological constitution. These things did not occur to him, not necessarily because they were known by him to be irrelevant to the facts under inquiry, but most likely because their consideration belongs to a level of analysis that normally falls outside the range of the historian's interests, and outside the scope of the historian's competence.

For convenience of reference, and for lack of better labels, let me call those phases of historical occurrences to which historians usually pay attention the "common-sense molar characteristics" of events; and let me refer to other characteristics of events which may be of possible causal relevance to their occurrence as "analytic molecular characteristics." I hasten to add that I realize this distinction to be a loose one, and that I know no way of sharpening it. Nevertheless, the distinction is a serviceable one, and permits me to state briefly why, as I see it, the actual explanations of human affairs will most likely continue to specify only some of the necessary conditions for the occurrence of events.

The point is that our customary formulations of common-sense molar characteristics are not only vague; they also cover an indefinite number of *specific variant forms* of such characteristics, which have never been exhaustively codified and catalogued in some systematic fashion. In consequence, only a statistical concomitance between common-sense molar traits can be reasonably expected. It is as if a physicist, after recognizing a gross distinction between metals and nonmetals, were to investigate the electrical conductivity of different objects without distinguishing further between different kinds of metals. Would it be surprising, in the light of what we know, if the generalizations he would then obtain about the variation of conductivity with, say, the temperature of metal objects, would be only statistical in form? Would we not agree that on such a level of analysis nothing more could be expected, and that to obtain more exact relations of dependence the physicist must refine his distinctions, and perhaps even undertake a detailed molecular analysis of his materials? On the other hand, the explanations which the historian usually offers for historical occurrences are in large measure controlled by those interests we all normally have in human affairs —interests which in a broad sense are practical, even if they are sometimes disinterested. I venture the opinion that if someone were to succeed in stating the sufficient conditions for Elizabeth's proclamation of her ambiguous title, but explained that occurrence in terms of analytic molecular characteristics—which included mention of, say, her detailed biological and genetic traits, the condition of her neural synapses, and the specific physical stimuli supplied by her environment—we would all turn away from such an account as not being the sort of history to which we are accustomed or in which we are interested. Accordingly, I see no genuine prospect for explanations in human history which will indeed state the necessary and sufficient conditions for the traits of events in which we are actually interested.

But it would certainly be unwarranted to conclude from all this that common-sense molar characteristics do not have determinate conditions for their occurrence. For it is conceivable that those conditions may need to be specified, at least in part, in terms of some analytic molecular characteristics. We are admittedly ignorant of just what the full complement of those conditions is; and even if there are in fact such conditions, it is possible that we shall never discover the complete set. On the other hand, the existence of sufficient conditions on some analytical molecular level of analysis cannot be excluded *a priori*. I therefore conclude that neither the *de facto* incomplete form of historical explanations, nor the restricted scope of our actual predictions of human events, is cogent evidence against determinism in history.

IV

I now turn to the argument which offers as ground for the rejection of determinism the production in the human scene of new ideas, novel modes of behavior, and unprecedented works of imagination and skill, and which attributes the unpredictability of human actions in part at least to the "creative advance of nature" manifested in the life of man.

The issues raised by this argument are identical with those associated with the doctrine of emergence; and I have time to discuss them only summarily. Two forms of this doctrine must be distinguished. The first form, which for convenience will be called "the doctrine of emergent levels," is atemporal. It maintains that many complex systems exhibit traits and modes of action which cannot be explained or predicted in terms of the properties that the component parts of those systems possess when not members of these systems. The second form of the doctrine, commonly known as "emergent evolution," is a temporal or historical thesis. It asserts that novel forms of organization appear in time, new traits are exhibited, and types of activities are manifested which did not previously exist, and which cannot be understood in terms of what had preceded them. I shall now argue that both versions of the doctrine of emergence are fully compatible with determinism.

Consider first a standard illustration for the thesis of emergent levels: the water molecule, many of whose traits are allegedly not predictable from the properties of its component hydrogen and oxygen atoms—that is, predictable neither from the properties of these atoms when they exist uncombined with other atoms, nor from the properties they possess in other chemical unions. Such formulations of illustrative examples are misleading, as could easily be shown. For the alleged "unpredictability" of emergent traits is not absolute, but is always relative to a particular theory that is adopted for the components of the systems exhibiting those emergent traits. For example, many properties of water are indeed emergents, relative to Dalton's theory of the atom; but some of these very properties are predictable, and hence not emergents, relative to the current quantum theory of atomic structure. But waiving this point, what do such examples of emergent levels really show? Do they establish the untenability of determinism? On the contrary, they clearly testify to the fact that, for example, certain distinctive properties of water come into existence only when hydrogen and oxygen atoms combine in a certain definite manner. More generally, the evidence seems to be overwhelming that even in those cases in which we cannot deduce the properties of complex wholes from the properties of their components, those complexes and their various traits come into existence or continue to exist only under determinate conditions.

The import of the doctrine of emergent evolution is essentially no different. There are various analytical and empirical difficulties which must be surmounted before many specific claims of the doctrine can be regarded as established. For example, criteria must be stated for judging whether two traits are "really" the same or different, as a preliminary to the empirical question whether one of them is temporally novel; indications must be given of the sort of evidence that is to be deemed relevant for supporting the frequently voiced claim that laws of nature themselves undergo change; and our present knowledge of the past must in many cases be enormously enlarged, if we are to assert with warrant that certain traits of events are temporally unprecedented. But despite such difficulties, no one can seriously question the main thesis that human beings are perennial sources of temporal novelties.

It must also be admitted that the emergence of many of these novelties could not have been predicted in advance. No one could have predicted the invention of the telephone prior to the work of Faraday and Henry; and no one could have predicted that Faraday was to make the scientific discoveries he did make. Nevertheless, there is nothing mysterious about the impossibility of such predictions, and the impossibility can indeed be shown to be a matter of formal logic. For to predict an event, the traits of that event must be formulated in a statement; and unless the predicates describing those traits occur in the premises of the predictive argument, that statement can follow from the premises neither deductively nor with any significant measure of probability. However, if some trait of an event is radically novel (and hence not definable in terms of previously existing traits), there will be no antecedently known regularities (or laws) connecting the former with the latter. In consequence, the predicate describing such a novel trait will not occur in any premises from which a predictive inference could be made. In short, our inability to predict a radically novel future is simply the consequence of a logical truism.

On the other hand, once a novel characteristic or novel object has come into existence, we are in the position to inquire, and often do inquire, into the conditions upon which the occurrence of that novelty is contingent. We may not always succeed in discovering those conditions, and we may perhaps never succeed in doing so in many cases. But we do not always fail entirely, nor is it just unintelligible to pursue such a quest.

Let me cite two examples of recent inquiries in this connection, though neither of them is especially favorable for my case. The sociology of science seeks, among other things, to ascertain the social conditions which are favorable to successful scientific research, as well as to the general acceptance of scientific discoveries. Its findings are thus far relatively meager; and given the level of analysis upon which its inquiries operate, it is hardly surprising that no sufficient conditions have yet been found for the occurrence or acceptance of a great scientific achievement. These inquiries have nevertheless established some things: for example, that a measure of free discussion and communication is a minimal requirement for progress in science, or that there are various necessary conditions, individual and social, for the occurrence of scientific innovations and their subsequent acceptance. Again, there has been some study of the psychology of creative thinking, directed to specifying the circumstances under which mathematicians, composers, and other inventive minds have achieved their creative successes. Here again the findings are slight. Certainly nothing has yet been discovered which would explain such remarkable feats as Mozart's writing of *The Magic Flute* or Newton's deduction of the Keplerian laws from gravitation theory; and it may well be that much more will have to be known about the genetic and physiological constitution of individual men, as well as about the effects of various types of environmental stimuli, before we can hope to account for even lesser achievements. But my point is that these diverse attempts at pushing back the frontiers of our ignorance are not inherently absurd, and that no antecedent limits can be fixed as to how far they may be pushed back. But the assumption of determinism in effect simply codifies our general objective as inquirers, to make those frontiers recede. To abandon that assumption would be tantamount to setting prescribed limits to inquiry itself.

V

The next argument against determinism I wish to consider is based on the claim that there is a fortuitous or chance element in history. But the word "chance" is far from univocal in the writings of historians and philosophers, and several of its more prominent senses must be distinguished.

In the first place, the word is frequently used to signify the absence of a pervasive and unified "design, plan, and order in human affairs," and in effect to deny that each historical event is relevantly related to every other. Those who employ "chance" in this sense clearly intend to controvert those philosophies of history already mentioned, which descry in the apparently chaotic happenings of the human scene the impress of some timeless Reason, or a unitary pattern of cumulative development. So used, the word obviously does not denote any agency or instrumentality that brings events into being, and in this sense it has no explanatory value whatsoever. On the other hand, it is also evident that on this meaning of "chance," the affirmation of chance happenings does not entail the denial of causal determinants for historical events, nor does such affirmation imply the futility of all inquiry into the conditions upon which specific historical occurrences may be contingent.

In the second place, "chance" is sometimes equated with "the unexpected and the unforeseen," where what is unforeseen may be a purely physical event or the social consequence of an action deliberately undertaken. Thus, the shift in the winds which contributed to the destruction of the Spanish Armada was apparently not anticipated by the Spaniards when they set sail for England. The disappearance of a slave economy in the United States, which seemed to many southern landowners to be part of the permanent social order, was not foreseen by most of them even as late as 1859. And few if any of those who contributed to the development of the internal combustion engine or to the production of moderately priced automobiles, envisaged in advance the enormous changes which resulted from these innovations in modes of urban and rural living, in individual and public morals, or in domestic politics and foreign relations. More generally, none of us can fully anticipate the unintended consequences of our choices and actions; and we are frequently inclined to label any striking departure from what is expected to happen normally as an "accident." However, "chance" in this sense is on the face of it but a name for our *de facto* ignorance. Clearly, the tenability of determinism is not being challenged when an event is designated as a "chance" occurrence in this meaning of the word.

In the third place, an event is often said to occur by chance if, to use a familiar formula, it occurs at the "intersection of two or more independent causal series." It is in this meaning of "chance" or "accident" that Bismarck is reported to have once remarked, after reflecting on the role of accident in ruining the plans of wise men, that there is a special providence for drunkards, fools, and the United States. For example, the military situation in 1781 during the American Revolutionary War made it imperative for Cornwallis to retreat from Yorktown. The disposition of the superior American and French forces prevented him from moving his troops by land, and he sought to escape by water. He did in fact transport some of his men across the York River, when a storm arose making the passage of the rest impossible—so that he was eventually compelled to surrender and in effect thereby to terminate the war. Commenting on these events, a recent historian remarks that "the atmospheric conditions that brought on the storm and the military conditions that caused Cornwallis's army to retreat were the products of altogether separate chains of causes and effects." (Oscar Handlin, *Change or Destiny*, p. 192.) Cornwallis's surrender is thus credited to chance, since it occurred at the juncture of two independent causal sequences—one of which was the chain of events that terminated in the distribution of the British and Franco-American forces, while the other was the different sequence which terminated in the storm. The two sequences themselves are said to be "independent," because no elements in either determined any elements in the other; and accordingly, the events in no one of the series determined the conjuncture consisting in the defeat of Cornwallis.

This notion of chance, as is well known, has an ancient lineage; and despite the unclarities that surround the metaphoric phrase "independent causal chains," it directs attention to the important if obvious point that while the occurrence of one phase of an event may be determined by one set of conditions, the latter may not suffice to determine some more inclusive phase of the event. But does it follow that an event which is the juncture of two independent causal lines is not determined at all? Does it even follow, as some writers have asserted, that the juncture "cannot be predicted from the laws determining any or all of the series"? These are patently gratuitous claims. For let us assume that an event is a "chance" occurrence in the present sense of the word—that is, it occurs at the juncture of several independent causal chains; then it is quite plain that the event *does* occur under the *determinate* conditions which are mentioned when the causal chains are specified at whose "intersection" the event lies. Moreover, it is surely a mistake to maintain that the point of juncture is *necessarily* unpredictable from the laws of "any or all the series," even if the detailed outcome of the juncture may not be predictable in *some* cases. A billiard ball moving along a given line under the impact of a blow from a cue, can certainly be predicted to collide with a steel ball travelling in the opposite direction along that line because of the presence of a strong magnet. More generally, and indeed more precisely, a statement asserting the occurrence of some event may not be deducible from either of two sets of premises; nevertheless, that statement may be deducible (and the event it describes predictable) from the logical conjunction of those sets of premises. Accordingly, to be a chance event in this sense of the word, is relative to the explanatory premises that happen to be adopted; and the characterization of an event as a chance occurrence is thus based on a purely logical distinction. But surely nothing in this distinction is prejudicial to the adequacy of the deterministic assumption.

There is one remaining sense of "chance" I want to note. According to it, an event happens by chance, if there are absolutely no determining conditions for its occurrence. *If* there are such events (or traits of events), they are not merely unexpected and unforeseen, but are *inherently* unforeseeable; and their occurrence could not be explained, even *after* they had happened, no matter how extensive our knowledge may become. It is, however, at best an unsettled question whether there *are* such chance events—and I venture this opinion despite the well-known rumor that it has been affirmatively settled by modern physics. For as I have already argued, such a question cannot, in the nature of the case, be answered definitively, since even repeated failure to find any causal conditions for some type of event can always be construed as evidence for human stupidity. Would we not ordinarily interpret a competent historian's readiness to label as "chance event" (in the present sense of the word) an occurrence which he is unable to explain, as simply an expression of his weariness or despair? On the other hand, if there are indeed chance events in this meaning of the word, there certainly is a definite limit to what can be explained. But since we cannot be sure for which specific events this limit is in force, we cannot be certain in connection with any of them that we really have an impregnable excuse for stopping our inquiries into their determinants.

VI

The final argument I must consider consists in the claim that imputation of genuine responsibility to human beings for any of their actions, is incompatible with a thoroughgoing determinism. I turn to this issue with a measure of dislike, for I would prefer not to stir up what ought to be dead ashes. If I nevertheless propose to discuss it, it is because the issue has been recently revived, not only by writers who make a career out of muddying clear waters, but also by sensitive thinkers of great acumen.

I shall take for my main text the recent book by Mr. Isaiah Berlin on *Historical Inevitability* (London and New York, 1954). This book is primarily a critique, and in my opinion a devastating critique, of philosophies of history which view the changes in human life as the unfolding of an inevitable destiny, and which therefore deny that human effort is of any avail in altering the ultimate course of events. However, Mr. Berlin also maintains that such philosophies are but the direct products of a consistent application of the deterministic assumption to human affairs. He therefore believes there are sufficient reasons for rejecting determinism, partly because it leads to such untenable philosophies of history, and partly because of several further difficulties he adduces. I shall ignore the former of these considerations, for I have already tried to show that determinism does not entail any doctrine of historical inevitability; and it is with Mr. Berlin's two additional arguments against determinism that I shall deal.

(1) Berlin takes his point of departure from the commonplace that an individual is morally responsible for an act he performs, only if the individual has not been coerced into doing it, and only if he has elected to do it of his own free volition. Accordingly, if a man is genuinely responsible for some act of his, he *could* have acted differently had his choice been different. So much perhaps everyone will be willing to grant. However, Mr. Berlin appears to hold that on the deterministic assumption (which he construes to deny that there are any areas of human life which cannot be exhaustively determined by law), the individual *could not* have chosen differently from the way he in fact did choose; he could not have done so, presumably because his choice at the time he made it was

determined by circumstances over which he had no control—circumstances such as his biological heritage, his character as formed by his previous actions, and the like. Mr. Berlin therefore maintains that on the deterministic premise, the supposition that a man could have chosen otherwise than he in fact did, is ultimately an illusion, resting on an ignorance of the facts. In consequence, Berlin concludes that determinism entails the elimination of individual responsibility, since it is not a man's *free* choice, but the conditions which determine his choice, that must be taken to explain a man's action. So Berlin declares:

> Nobody denies that it would be stupid as well as cruel to blame me for not being taller than I am, or to regard the color of my hair or the qualities of my intellect or my heart as being due principally to my own free choice; these attributes are as they are through no decision of mine. If I extend this category without limit, then whatever is, is necessary and inevitable. . . . To blame and praise, consider possible alternative courses of action, damn or congratulate historical figures for acting as they do or did, becomes an absurd activity. (p. 26.)

And he adds:

> If I were convinced that although choices did affect what occurred, yet they were themselves wholly determined by factors not within the individual's control (including his own motives and springs of action), I should certainly not regard him as morally praiseworthy or blameworthy. (pp. 26–27, footnote.)

I have two comments to make on this. (a) In the first place, it is difficult to obtain a clear idea of the notion of the human self with which Mr. Berlin operates. For on his view, the human self is apparently not only to be distinguished from the human body, but also from any of the choices an individual makes—insofar as a choice is dependent on a man's dispositions, motives, and springs of action.

Now no doubt, when I deliberate and finally seem to choose between alternatives, I am usually not aware that the choice may be the expression of a set of more or less stable dispositions, more transient impulses, and the like—any more than I am usually aware of my heartbeat or of the organ which produces it. But should I become aware of these things, as I sometimes am aware, does my choice or my heart cease to be mine? If I understand Mr. Berlin, he requires me to answer in the negative, though for no obviously good reason. On the contrary, he appears to have an irresolvable puzzle on his hands of how to identify the human self—a puzzle that arises from his so construing the nature of that self, that any trait or action which stands in relations of causal dependence to anything whatever, is automatically cut off from being a genuine phase of the self. It is as if a physicist in analyzing the performance of a baseball, and noting that the shape, the surface quality, and the elastic properties of the ball are partly determinative of its behavior when it is struck by a bat, were to declare that these traits do not properly belong to the ball, but are as much external to it as the impulse imparted by the bat. Just how and where the boundaries of the individual human self are drawn, may vary with different contexts of self-identification, and there may even be important cultural differences in this respect. But however they are drawn, they must not be so drawn that nothing finally can be identified as the self. They must not be so drawn that an insoluble puzzle is made of the fact that we conceive ourselves to be acting freely (*i.e.*, without external constraints), even though we may recognize that some of our choices are the products of our dispositions, our past actions, and our present impulses.

(b) This brings me to my second comment. Mr. Berlin's argument seems to be unwittingly patterned on the model used so typically by Eddington—namely, that since physics analyzes common-sense objects like tables into a large number of rapidly moving minute particles, with relatively large distances between them, it is therefore illusory to regard tables as hard solids with continuous surfaces. This argument is fallacious, as has often been noted, and involves among other things a confusion of types or categories. In any event, it does not follow that because terms like "solid," "hard," and "continuous" are not applicable in their ordinary senses to a cloud of molecules, they are therefore not correctly applicable to macroscopic objects like tables.

But Mr. Berlin's argument suffers from a similar flaw. For it is a similar mistake to claim that men cannot be genuinely responsible for any of their acts, just because there are conditions inherent in the biological and psychological structure of the human body, under which such responsibility is manifested. Now it is an empirical fact, as well attested as any, that men often do deliberate and decide between alternatives; and whatever we have discovered, or may in the future discover, about the conditions under which men deliberate and choose, cannot be taken, on pain of a fatal incoherence, as evidence for *denying* that such deliberative choices *do* occur.

On the other hand, the imputation of responsibility is an empirically controllable matter, and we may be mistaken in some of the imputations we make. We may discover, for example, that an individual continues to be a petty thief, despite our best efforts to educate him by way of praise and blame, rewards and punishments, and despite his own apparently serious attempts to mend his ways. We may then conclude that the individual suffers from a mild derangement and cannot control certain of his acts. In such a case, the imputation of responsibility to that individual for those acts would be misplaced. But the fact nevertheless remains that the distinction between acts over which a man does have control and those over which he does not, is not thereby impugned—even if we should discover that there are conditions under which the capacity for such control is manifested and acquired. In short, an individual is correctly characterized as a responsible moral agent, if he behaves in the manner in which a normal moral agent behaves; and he is correctly characterized in this way, even if all the conditions which make it possible for him to function as a moral agent at some given time are not within his control on that occasion.

(2) But Mr. Berlin has one further argument against determinism, upon which he apparently sets great store. He claims that irrespective of the truth of determinism, belief in it does not color the ordinary thoughts of the majority of men. If it did, so he argues, the language we employ in making moral distinctions and in expressing moral suasions would not be what it actually is. For this language in its customary meaning tacitly assumes that men are free to choose and to act *differently* from the way they *actually* choose and act. But if determinism were sound and we really believed in it, Mr. Berlin therefore concludes, our ordinary moral distinctions would not be applicable to anything, and our moral experience would be unintelligible.

Mr. Berlin puts his case as follows:

> If determinism were a valid theory of human behavior, these distinc-
> tions [like "you should not (or need not) have done this," and "I
> could do it, but I would rather not," which plainly involve the no-
> tion of more than the merely logical possibility of the realization of
> alternatives other than those which were in fact realized, namely of
> differences between situations in which individuals can be reasonably
> regarded as being responsible for their acts, and those in which they
> cannot] would be as inappropriate as the attribution of moral re-
> sponsibility to the planetary system or the tissues of a living cell. . . .
> Unless we attach some meaning to the notion of free acts—that is,
> acts not wholly determined by antecedent events or by the nature
> and "dispositional characteristics" of either persons or things, it is
> difficult to see how we come to distinguish acts to which responsibil-
> ity is attached from mere segments in a physical, psychical, or psycho-
> physical causal chain of events. . . . If the determinist hypothesis
> were true, and adequately accounted for the actual world, there is a
> clear sense in which (despite all the extraordinary casuistry which
> has been employed to avoid this conclusion) the notion of human
> responsibility, as ordinarily understood would no longer apply to any
> actual, but only to imaginary or conceivable, states of affairs. . . .
> To speak, as some theorists of history (and scientists with a philo-
> sophical bent) tend to do, as if one might accept the determinist
> hypothesis, and yet to continue to think and speak much as we do at
> present, is to breed intellectual confusion. (pp. 32–33.)

I have already examined those parts of this critique which, as I
see it, thoroughly confound the notion of "free acts" with that of
"determined acts"; and my readers must decide where the real
intellectual confusion is to be found. But I do want to consider
whether, as Mr. Berlin claims, a consistent determinist cannot
employ ordinary moral discourse in its customary meanings.

(a) Is this claim to be decided on the basis of straightforward
empirical evidence, as Berlin sometimes hints it ought to be? If so,
then although no statistical data are available and the available
information is doubtless not conclusive, the evidence we do have
does not appear to support his contention. The language of many
devout religious believers, to say nothing of philosophers like
Spinoza, provides some ground for maintaining that many men
find no psychological obstacles to making normal moral appraisals,
despite their explicit and apparently wholehearted adherence to a

thoroughgoing determinism. I cite one instance out of a large number that could be mentioned. As is well known, Bishop Bossuet composed his *Discourse on Universal History* with the intent to offer guidance to the Dauphin on the proper conduct of a royal prince. In it, however, he maintained that

> the long concatenation of particular causes which make and undo empires depends on the decrees of Divine Providence. High up in His heavens God holds the reins of all kingdoms. He has every heart in His hand. Sometimes He restrains passions, sometimes He leaves them free, and thus agitates mankind. By this means God carries out His redoubtable judgments according to ever infallible rules. He is it who prepares results through the most distant causes, and who strikes vast blows whose repercussion is so wide spread. Thus it is that God reigns over all nations.
>
> (*Discourse on Universal History*, Part XIV, Chap. viii; quoted by G. J. Renier, *History: Its Purpose and Method*, p. 261.)

The relevant question to ask at this point is not whether Bossuet was sound in his claims, nor whether he was correct in holding that the reconciliation of human freedom with the operation of a Divine Providence is a transcendent mystery. The relevant question is whether Bossuet did in fact subscribe to a Providential (and therefore deterministic) conception of history, and yet employ ordinary moral language to express familiar moral distinctions. There seems to me little doubt that the answer is clearly affirmative, contrary to Mr. Berlin's assumption that the answer ought to be negative.

(b) Let us suppose, however, that Mr. Berlin is right in claiming that if we really did come to believe in a thoroughgoing determinism, the meanings of our moral discourse would be altered. But just what would this assumed fact establish? There are indeed comparable cases in other domains of thought in which, because of the influence of new theoretical ideas, the meanings of older but surviving locutions have to some extent been revised. Thus, most educated men today accept the heliocentric theory of planetary motions, but continue to use the language of the sun rising and setting; and it is safe to suppose that they do not associate with such locutions the precise meanings those expressions doubtless had when the Ptolemaic theory was dominant. Nevertheless, some of the distinctions which this older language codified are not without foundation even today, for in many contexts of observation and analysis it is not incorrect to describe the facts by saying that the sun rises in the east and sinks in the west; and we have learned to use this language so as to express these distinctions, without committing ourselves to a number of others that depend on an acceptance of a geocentric theory of the heavens.

Analogously, however, should the majority of men accept the deterministic assumptions—perhaps because all human acts had in fact been discovered to have determinate conditions for their occurrence —the difference would not thereby be wiped out between those acts which we now describe in our current language as freely chosen and those acts which are not, between those traits of character and personality over which an individual manifestly has control and those over which he has not. When the assumed shifts in linguistic meanings are completed, moreover, it still will be the case that certain types of acts will be affected by praise and blame, that men will continue to be able to control and modify by suitable discipline some of their impulses but not others, that some men will be able by making the effort to improve certain of their performances while other men will not be able to do so, and so on. To deny this, and to maintain the contrary, is to suppose that men would be transformed, by a mere change in theoretical belief, into creatures radically different from what they were prior to that alteration in belief; and such a supposition is hardly credible. But if such a supposition is rejected, our ordinary moral language with its associated customary meanings will survive at least partially a general acceptance of the deterministic assumption. Belief in determinism is therefore not incompatible, either psychologically or logically, with the normal use of moral discourse or with the significant imputation of moral responsibility. The alleged incompatibility can be established, so it seems to me, only if the question-begging premise is introduced that our making moral distinctions at all entails disbelief in determinism.

Let me say in conclusion what I have already asserted earlier. I do not believe that determinism is a demonstrable thesis, and I think that if it is construed as a statement about a categorical feature of everything whatsoever it may even be false. I have spent much time in this paper defending it against various types of criticism because, were those criticisms mistakenly accepted as sound, there would be a strong likelihood that premature limits would be set on the possible scope of scientific inquiry. For on my construction of determinism, it is in effect a regulative principle which formulates the general objective of science as a search for explanations—as a quest for ascertaining the conditions upon which the occurrence of events is contingent. I do not wish to disguise the fact that the dogmatic adoption of various *special* forms of the deterministic principle has often hindered the advance of knowledge, or that much iniquitous social practice and much doubtful social theory has been defended in the name of *particular* versions of determinism. Nevertheless, to abandon the deterministic principle itself, is to withdraw from the enterprise of science. And I do not believe that however acute is our awareness of the rich variety of human experience, and however sensitive our concern for the fuller development of human individuality, our best interests will be served by stopping objective inquiry into the various conditions which determine the existence of human traits and actions, and by thus shutting the door to the progressive liberation from illusion that can come from the achievement of such knowledge.

WHAT IS FREE WILL AND IS IT TRUE?

THOMAS REID

Some Arguments For Free Will

The modern advocates for the doctrine of necessity lay the stress of their cause upon the influence of motives.

"Every deliberate action," they say, "must have a motive. When there is no motive on the other side, this motive must determine the agent: when there are contrary motives, the strongest must prevail: we reason from men's motives to their actions, as we do from other causes to their effects: if man be a free agent, and be not governed by motives, all his actions must be mere caprice, rewards and punishments can have no effect, and such a being must be absolutely ungovernable."

In order therefore to understand distinctly, in what sense we ascribe moral liberty to man, it is necessary to understand what influence we allow to motives. To prevent misunderstanding, which has been very common upon this point, I offer the following observations. First, I grant that all rational beings are influenced, and ought to be influenced by motives. But the influence of motives is of a very different nature from that of efficient causes. They are neither causes nor agents. They suppose an efficient cause, and can do nothing without it. We cannot, without absurdity, suppose a motive, either to act, or to be acted upon; it is equally incapable of action and of passion; because it is not a thing that exists, but a thing that is conceived; it is what the schoolmen called an *ens rationis*. Motives, therefore, may *influence* to action, but they do

* From *The Works of Thomas Reid,* published by Samuel Etheridge, Jr., 1815.

not act. They may be compared to advice, or exhortation, which leaves a man still at liberty. For in vain is advice given when there is not a power either to do, or to forbear, what it recommends. In like manner, motives suppose liberty in the agent, otherwise they have no influence at all.

It is a law of nature, with respect to matter, that every motion, and change of motion, is proportional to the force impressed, and in the direction of that force. The scheme of necessity supposes a similar law to obtain in all the actions of intelligent beings; which, with little alteration, may be expressed thus: every action, or change of action, in an intelligent being, is proportional to the force of motives impressed, and in the direction of that force.

The law of nature respecting matter, is grounded upon this principle, that matter is an inert, inactive substance, which does not act, but is acted upon; and the law of necessity must be grounded upon the supposition, that an intelligent being is an inert, inactive substance, which does not act, but is acted upon.

Secondly, Rational beings, in proportion as they are wise and good, will act according to the best motives; and every rational being who does otherwise, abuses his liberty. The most perfect being, in every thing where there is a right and a wrong, a better and a worse, always infallibly acts according to the best motives. This indeed is little else than an identical proposition: for it is a contradiction to say, that a perfect being does what is wrong or unreasonable. But to say, that he does not act freely, because he always does what is best, is to say, that the proper use of liberty destroys liberty, and that liberty consists only in its abuse.

The moral perfection of the Deity consists, not in having no power to do ill, otherwise, as Dr. Clark justly observes, there would be no ground to thank him for his goodness to us any more than for his eternity or immensity; but his moral perfection consists in this, that, when he has power to do every thing, a power which cannot be resisted, he exerts that power only in doing what is wisest and best. To be subject to necessity is to have no power at all; for power and necessity are opposites. We grant, therefore, that motives have influence, similar to that of advice or persuasion; but this influence is perfectly consistent with liberty, and indeed supposes liberty.

Thirdly, Whether every deliberate action must have a motive, depends on the meaning we put upon the word *deliberate*. If, by a deliberate action, we mean an action wherein motives are weighed, which seems to be the original meaning of the word, surely there must be motives, and contrary motives, otherwise they could not be weighed. But if a deliberate action means only, as it commonly does, an action done by a cool and calm determination of the mind, with forethought and will, I believe there are innumerable such actions done without a motive.

This must be appealed to every man's consciousness. I do many trifling actions every day, in which, upon the most careful reflection, I am conscious of no motive; and to say that I may be influenced by a motive of which I am not conscious, is, in the first place, an arbitrary supposition without any evidence, and then, it is to say, that I may be convinced by an argument which never entered into my thought.

Cases frequently occur, in which an end, that is of some importance, may be answered equally well by any one of several different means. In such cases, a man who intends the end finds not the least difficulty in taking one of these means, though he be firmly persuaded, that it has no title to be preferred to any of the others.

To say that this is a case that cannot happen, is to contradict the experience of mankind; for surely a man who has occasion to lay out a shilling, or a guinea, may have two hundred that are of equal value, both to the giver and to the receiver, any one of which will answer his purpose equally well. To say, that, if such a case should happen, the man could not execute his purpose, is still more ridiculous, though it have the authority of some of the schoolmen, who determined, that the ass, between two equal bundles of hay, would stand still till it died of hunger.

If a man could not act without a motive, he would have no power at all; for motives are not in our power; and he that has not power over a necessary mean, has not power over the end.

That an action, done without any motive, can neither have merit nor demerit, is much insisted on by the writers for necessity, and triumphantly, as if it were the very hinge of the controversy. I grant it to be a self-evident proposition, and I know no author that ever denied it.

How insignificant soever, in moral estimation, the actions may be which are done without any motive, they are of moment in the question concerning moral liberty. For, if there ever was any action of this kind, motives are not the sole causes of human actions. And if we have the power of acting without a motive, that power, joined to a weaker motive, may counterbalance a stronger.

Fourthly, It can never be proved, that when there is a motive on one side only, that motive must determine the action.

According to the laws of reasoning, the proof is incumbent on those who hold the affirmative; and I have never seen a shadow of argument, which does not take for granted the thing in question, to wit, that motives are the sole causes of actions.

Is there no such thing as willfulness, caprice or obstinacy, among mankind? If there be not, it is wonderful that they should have names in all languages. If there be such things, a single motive, or even many motives, may be resisted.

Fifthly, When it is said, that of contrary motives the strongest always prevails, this can neither be affirmed nor denied with understanding, until we know distinctly what is meant by the strongest motive.

I do not find, that those who have advanced this as a self-evident axiom, have ever attempted to explain what they mean by the strongest motive, or have given any rule by which we may judge which of two motives is the strongest.

How shall we know whether the strongest motive always prevails, if we know not which is strongest? There must be some test by which their strength is to be tried, some balance in which they may be weighed, otherwise, to say that the strongest motive always prevails, is to speak without any meaning. We must therefore search for this test, or balance, since they who have laid so much stress upon this axiom, have left us wholly in the dark as to its meaning. I grant, that when the contrary motives are of the same kind, and differ only in quantity, it may be easy to say which is the strongest. Thus a bribe of a thousand pounds is a stronger motive than a bribe of a hundred pounds. But when the motives are of different kinds, as money and fame, duty and worldly interest, health and strength, riches and honor, by what rule shall we judge which is the strongest motive?

Either we measure the strength of motives, merely by their prevalence, or by some other standard distinct from their prevalence.

If we measure their strength merely by their prevalence, and by the strongest motive mean only the motive that prevails, it will be true indeed that the strongest motive prevails; but the proposition will be identical, and mean no more than that the strongest motive is the strongest motive. From this surely no conclusion can be drawn.

If it should be said, that by the strength of a motive is not meant its prevalence, but the cause of its prevalence; that we measure the cause by the effect, and from the superiority of the effect conclude the superiority of the cause, as we conclude that to be the heaviest weight which bears down the scale: I answer, that, according to this explication of the axiom, it takes for granted that motives are the causes, and the sole causes of actions. Nothing is left to the agent, but to be acted upon by the motives, as the balance is by the weights. The axiom supposes, that the agent does not act, but is acted upon; and, from this supposition, it is concluded that he does not act. This is to reason in a circle, or rather it is not reasoning but begging the question.

Contrary motives may very properly be compared to advocates pleading the opposite sides of a cause at the bar. It would be very weak reasoning to say, that such an advocate is the most powerful pleader, because sentence was given on his side. The sentence is in the power of the judge, not of the advocate. It is equally weak reasoning, in proof of necessity, to say, such a motive prevailed, therefore it is the strongest; since the defenders of liberty maintain that the determination was made by the man, and not by the motive.

We are therefore brought to this issue, that unless some measure of the strength of motives can be found distinct from their prevalence, it cannot be determined, whether the strongest motive always prevails or not. If such a measure can be found and applied, we may be able to judge of the truth of this maxim, but not otherwise.

* *

We have, by our constitution, a natural conviction or belief that we act freely. A conviction so early, so universal, and so necessary in most of our rational operations, that it must be the result of our constitution, and the work of Him that made us.

Some of the most strenuous advocates for the doctrine of necessity acknowledge, that it is impossible to act upon it. They say that we have a natural sense or conviction that we act freely, but that this is a fallacious sense.

This doctrine is dishonorable to our Maker, and lays a foundation for universal skepticism. It supposes the Author of our being to have given us one faculty on purpose to deceive us, and another by which we may detect the fallacy, and find that he imposed upon us.

If any one of our natural faculties be fallacious, there can be no reason to trust any of them; for he that made one made all.

The genuine dictate of our natural faculties is the voice of God, no less than what he reveals from heaven; and to say that it is fallacious, is to impute a lie to the God of truth.

If candour and veracity be not an essential part of moral excellence, there is no such thing as moral excellence, nor any reason to rely on the declarations and promises of the Almighty. A man may be tempted to lie, but not without being conscious of guilt and of meanness. Shall we impute to the Almighty what we cannot impute to a man without a heinous affront?

Passing this opinion, therefore, as shocking to an ingenuous mind, and, in its consequences, subversive of all religion, all morals, and all knowledge, let us proceed to consider the evidence of our having a natural conviction that we have some degree of active power.

The very conception or idea of active power must be derived from something in our own constitution. It is impossible to account for it otherwise. We see events, but we see not the power that produces them. We perceive one event to follow another, but we perceive not the chain that binds them together. The notion of power and causation, therefore, cannot be got from external objects.

Yet the notion of causes, and the belief that every event must have a cause which had power to produce it, is found in every human mind so firmly established, that it cannot be rooted out.

This notion and this belief must have its origin from something in our constitution; and that it is natural to man, appears from the following observations.

First, We are conscious of many voluntary exertions, some easy, others more difficult, some requiring a great effort. These are exertions of power. And though a man may be unconscious of his power when he does not exert it, he must have both the conception and the belief of it, when he knowingly and willingly exerts it, with intention to produce some effect.

Secondly, Deliberation about an action of moment, whether we shall do it or not, implies a conviction that it is in our power. To deliberate about an end, we must be convinced that the means are in our power; and to deliberate about the means, we must be convinced that we have power to choose the most proper.

Thirdly, Suppose our deliberation brought to an issue, and that we resolved to do what appeared proper, can we form such a resolution or purpose, without any conviction of power to execute it? No; it is impossible. A man cannot resolve to lay out a sum of money, which he neither has, nor hopes ever to have.

Fourthly, Again, when I plight my faith in any promise or contract, I must believe that I shall have power to perform what I promise. Without this persuasion, a promise would be downright fraud.

There is a condition implied in every promise, *if we live,* and *if God continue with us the power which he has given us.* Our conviction, therefore, of this power derogates not in the least from our dependence upon God. The rudest savage is taught by nature to admit this condition in all promises, whether it be expressed or not. For it is a dictate of common sense, that we can be under no obligation to do what it is impossible for us to do.

If we act upon the system of necessity, there must be another condition implied in all deliberation, in every resolution, and in every promise; and that is, *if we shall be willing.* But the will not being in our power, we cannot engage for it.

If this condition be understood, as it must be understood if we act upon the system of necessity, there can be no deliberation or resolution, nor any obligation in a promise. A man might as well deliberate, resolve, and promise, upon the actions of other men as upon his own.

It is no less evident, that we have a conviction of power in other men, when we advise, or persuade, or command, or conceive them to be under obligation by their promises.

Fifthly, Is it possible for any man to blame himself for yielding to necessity? Then he may blame himself for dying, or for being a man. Blame supposes a wrong use of power; and when a man does as well as it was possible for him to do, wherein is he to be blamed? Therefore all conviction of wrong conduct, all remorse and self-condemnation, imply a conviction of our power to have done better. Take away this conviction, and there may be a sense of misery, or a dread of evil to come, but there can be no sense of guilt, or resolution to do better.

Many who hold the doctrine of necessity, disown these consequences of it, and think to evade them. To such they ought not to be imputed; but their inseparable connection with that doctrine appears self-evident; and therefore some late patrons of it have had the boldness to avow them. "They cannot accuse themselves of having done any thing wrong in the ultimate sense of the words. In a strict sense, they have nothing to do with repentance, confession, and pardon, these being adapted to a fallacious view of things."

Those who can adopt these sentiments, may indeed celebrate, with high encomiums, *the great and glorious doctrine of necessity*. It restores them, in their own conceit, to the state of innocence. It delivers them from all the pangs of guilt and remorse, and from all fear about their future conduct, though not about their fate. They may be as secure that they shall do nothing wrong, as those who have finished their course. A doctrine so flattering to the mind of a sinner, is very apt to give strength to weak arguments.

After all, it is acknowledged by those who boast of this glorious doctrine, "That every man, let him use what efforts he can, will necessarily feel the sentiments of shame, remorse, and repentance, and, oppressed with a sense of guilt, will have recourse to that mercy of which he stands in need."

The meaning of this seems to me to be, that although the doctrine of necessity be supported by invincible arguments, and though it be the most consolatory doctrine in the world; yet no man in his most serious moments, when he sits himself before the throne of his Maker, can possibly believe it, but must then necessarily lay aside this glorious doctrine, and all its flattering consequences, and return to the humiliating conviction of his having made a bad use of the power which God had given him.

If the belief of our having active power be necessarily implied in those rational operations we have mentioned, it must be coeval with our reason; it must be as universal among men, and as necessary in the conduct of life, as those operations are.

We cannot recollect by memory when it began. It cannot be a prejudice of education, or of false philosophy. It must be a part of our constitution, or the necessary result of our constitution, and therefore the work of God.

It resembles, in this respect, our belief of the existence of a material world; our belief that those we converse with are living and intelligent beings; our belief that those things did really happen which we distinctly remember, and our belief that we continue the same identical persons.

We find difficulty in accounting for our belief of these things; and some philosophers think, that they have discovered good reasons for throwing it off. But it sticks fast, and the greatest skeptic finds, that he must yield to it in his practice, while he wages war with it in speculation.

If it be objected to this argument, that the belief of our acting freely cannot be implied in the operations we have mentioned, because those operations are performed by them who believe that we are, in all our actions, governed by necessity; the answer to this objection is, that men in their practice may be governed by a belief which in speculation they reject.

However strange and unaccountable this may appear, there are many well-known instances of it.

I knew a man who was as much convinced as any man of the folly of the popular belief of apparitions in the dark, yet he could not sleep in a room alone, nor go alone into a room in the dark. Can it be said, that his fear did not imply a belief of danger? This is impossible. Yet his philosophy convinced him, that he was in no more danger in the dark when alone, than with company.

Here an unreasonable belief, which was merely a prejudice of the nursery, stuck so fast as to govern his conduct, in opposition to his speculative belief as a philosopher, and a man of sense.

There are few persons who can look down from the battlement of a very high tower without fear, while their reason convinces them that they are in no more danger than when standing upon the ground.

There have been persons who professed to believe that there is no distinction between virtue and vice, yet in their practice, they resented injuries, and esteemed noble and virtuous actions.

There have been skeptics who professed to disbelieve their senses, and every human faculty; but no skeptic was ever known, who did not, in practice, pay a regard to his senses and to his other faculties.

There are some points of belief so necessary, that, without them, a man would not be the being which God made him. These may be opposed in speculation, but it is impossible to root them out. In a speculative hour they seem to vanish, but in practice they resume their authority. This seems to be the case of those who hold the doctrine of necessity, and yet act as if they were free.

This natural conviction of some degree of power in ourselves and in other men, respects voluntary actions only. For as all our power is directed by our will, we can form no conception of power, properly so called, that is not under the direction of will. And therefore our exertions, our deliberations, our purposes, our promises, are only in things that depend upon our will. Our advices, exhortations, and commands, are only in things that depend upon the will of those to whom they are addressed. We impute no guilt to ourselves, nor to others, in things where the will is not concerned.

But it deserves our notice, that we do not conceive every thing, without exception to be in a man's power which depends upon his will. There are many exceptions to this general rule. The most obvious of these I shall mention, because they both serve to illustrate the rule, and are of importance in the question concerning the liberty of man.

In the rage of madness, men are absolutely deprived of the power of self-government. They act voluntarily, but their will is driven as by a tempest, which, in lucid intervals, they resolve to oppose with all their might, but are overcome when the fit of madness returns.

Idiots are like men walking in the dark, who cannot be said to have the power of choosing their way, because they cannot distinguish the good road from the bad. Having no light in their understanding, they must either sit still, or be carried on by some blind impulse.

Between the darkness of infancy, which is equal to that of idiots, and the maturity of reason, there is a long twilight which, by insensible degrees, advances to the perfect day.

In this period of life, man has but little of the power of self-government. His actions, by nature, as well as by the laws of society, are in the power of others more than in his own. His folly and indiscretion, his levity and inconstancy, are considered as the fault of youth, rather than of the man. We consider him as half a man and half a child, and expect that each by turns should play its part. He would be thought a severe and unequitable censor of manners, who required the same cool deliberation, the same steady conduct, and the same mastery over himself in a boy of thirteen, as in a man of thirty.

It is an old adage, that violent anger is a short fit of madness. If this be literally true in any case, a man in such a fit of passion, cannot be said to have the command of himself. If real madness could be proved, it must have the effect of madness while it lasts, whether it be for an hour or for life. But the madness of a short fit of passion, if it be really madness, is incapable of proof; and therefore it is not admitted in human tribunals as an exculpation. And, I believe, there is no case where a man can satisfy his own mind that his passion, both in its beginning and in its progress, was irresistible. The Searcher of hearts alone knows infallibly what allowance is due in cases of this kind.

But a violent passion, though it may not be irresistible, is difficult to be resisted: and a man, surely, has not the same power over himself in passion, as when he is cool. On this account it is allowed by all men to alleviate, when it cannot exculpate; and has its weight in criminal courts, as well as in private judgment.

It ought likewise to be observed, that he who has accustomed himself to restrain his passions, enlarges by habit his power over them, and consequently over himself. When we consider that a Canadian savage can acquire the power of defying death, in its most dreadful forms, and of braving the most exquisite torment for many long hours, without losing the command of himself; we may learn from this, that, in the constitution of human nature, there is ample scope for the enlargement of that power of self-command, without which there can be no virtue nor magnanimity.

There are cases, however, in which a man's voluntary actions are thought to be very little, if at all, in his power, on account of the violence of the motive that impels him. The magnanimity of a hero, or of a martyr, is not expected in every man, and on all occasions.

If a man trusted by the government with a secret, which it is high treason to disclose, be prevailed upon by a bribe, we have no mercy for him, and hardly allow the greatest bribe to be any alleviation of his crime.

But, on the other hand, if the secret be extorted by the rack, or by the dread of present death, we pity him more than we blame him, and would think it severe and unequitable to condemn him as a traitor.

What is the reason that all men agree in condemning this man as a traitor in the first case, and in the last, either exculpate him, or think his fault greatly alleviated? If he acted necessarily in both cases, compelled by an irresistible motive, I can see no reason why we should not pass the same judgment on both.

But the reason of these different judgments is evidently this, that the love of money, and of what is called a man's interest, is a cool motive, which leaves to a man the entire power over himself; but the torment of the rack, or the dread of present death, are so violent motives, that men who have not uncommon strength of mind, are not masters of themselves in such a situation, and therefore what they do is not imputed, or is thought less criminal.

If a man resist such motives, we admire his fortitude, and think his conduct heroical rather than human. If he yields, we impute it to human frailty, and think him rather to be pitied than severely censured.

Inveterate habits are acknowledged to diminish very considerably the power a man has over himself. Although we may think him highly blameable in acquiring them, yet when they are confirmed to a certain degree, we consider him as no longer master of himself, and hardly reclaimable without a miracle.

Thus we see, that the power which we are led by common sense to ascribe to man, respects his voluntary actions only, and that it has various limitations even with regard to them. Some actions that depend upon our will are easy, others very difficult, and some, perhaps, beyond our power. In different men, the power of self-government is different, and in the same man at different times. It may be diminished, or perhaps lost, by bad habits; it may be greatly increased by good habits.

These are facts attested by experience, and supported by the common judgment of mankind. Upon the system of liberty, they are perfectly intelligible; but, I think, irreconcileable to that of necessity; for, how can there be an easy and a difficult in actions equally subject to necessity? or, how can power be greater or less, increased or diminished, in those who have no power?

This natural conviction of our acting freely, which is acknowledged by many who hold the doctrine of necessity, ought to throw the whole burden of proof upon that side: for, by this, the side of liberty has what lawyers call a *jus quæsitum*, or a right of ancient possession, which ought to stand good till it be overturned. If it cannot be proved that we always act from necessity, there is no need of arguments on the other side, to convince us that we are free agents.

To illustrate this by a similar case: if a philosopher would persuade me, that my fellow men with whom I converse, are not thinking intelligent beings, but mere machines; though I might be at a loss to find arguments against this strange opinion, I should think it reasonable to hold the belief which nature gave me before I was capable of weighing evidence, until convincing proof is brought against it.

C. A. CAMPBELL

Has the Self "Free Will"?

Let me, then, briefly sum up the answer at which we have arrived to our question about the kind of freedom required to justify moral responsibility. It is that a man can be said to exercise free will in a morally significant sense only in so far as his chosen act is one of which he is the sole cause or author, and only if—in the straightforward, categorical sense of the phrase—he "could have chosen otherwise."

I confess that this answer is in some ways a disconcerting one, disconcerting, because most of us, however objective we are in the actual conduct of our thinking, would *like* to be able to believe that moral responsibility is real: whereas the freedom required for moral responsibility, on the analysis we have given, is certainly far more difficult to establish than the freedom required on the analyses we found ourselves obliged to reject. If, for example, moral freedom entails only that I could have acted otherwise *if* I had chosen otherwise, there is no real "problem" about it at all. I am "free" in the normal case where there is no external obstacle to prevent my translating the alternative choice into action, and not free in other cases. Still less is there a problem if all that moral freedom entails is that

* From C. A. Campbell, Lecture IX, "Has the Self 'Free Will'?" in *On Selfhood and Godhood* (London: George Allen & Unwin Ltd., 1957). Reprinted by permission of the publishers.

I could have acted otherwise *if* I had been a differently constituted person, or been in different circumstances. Clearly I am *always* free in *this* sense of freedom. But, as I have argued, these so-called "freedoms" fail to give us the pre-conditions of moral responsibility, and hence leave the freedom of the traditional free-will problem, the freedom that people are really concerned about, precisely where it was.

.   .   .   .

That brings me to the second, and more constructive, part of this lecture. From now on I shall be considering whether it is reasonable to believe that man does in fact possess a free will. . . . If so, just how and where within the complex fabric of the volitional life are we to locate it?—for although free will must presumably belong (if anywhere) to the volitional side of human experience, it is pretty clear from the way in which we have been forced to define it that it does not pertain simply to volition as such; not even to all volitions that are commonly dignified with the name of "choices." It has been, I think, one of the more serious impediments to profitable discussion of the Free Will problem that Libertarians and Determinists alike have so often failed to appreciate the comparatively narrow area within which the free will that is necessary to "save" morality is required to operate. It goes without saying that this failure has been gravely prejudicial to the case for Libertarianism. I attach a good deal of importance, therefore, to the problem of locating free will correctly within the volitional orbit. Its solution forestalls and annuls, I believe, some of the more tiresome clichés of Determinist criticism.

We saw earlier that Common Sense's practice of "making allowances" in its moral judgments for the influence of heredity and environment indicates Common Sense's conviction, both that a just moral judgment must discount determinants of choice over which the agent has no control, and also (since it still accepts moral judgments as legitimate) that *something* of moral relevance survives which can be regarded as genuinely self-originated. We are now to try to discover what this "something" is. And I think we may still usefully take Common Sense as our guide. Suppose one asks the ordinary intelligent citizen *why* he deems it proper to make allowances for X, whose heredity and/or environment are unfortunate. He will tend to reply, I think, in some such terms as these: that X has more and stronger temptations to deviate from what is right than Y or Z, who are normally circumstanced, so that he must put forth *a stronger moral effort* if he is to achieve the same level of external conduct. The intended implication seems to be that X is just as morally praiseworthy as Y or Z *if* he exerts an equivalent moral effort, even though he may not thereby achieve an equal success in conforming his will to the "concrete" demands of duty. And this implies, again, Common Sense's belief that in *moral effort* we have something for which a man is responsible *without qualification,* something that is *not* affected by heredity and environment but depends *solely* upon the self itself.

Now in my opinion Common Sense has here, in principle, hit upon the one and only defensible answer. Here, and here alone, so far as I can see, in the act of deciding whether to put forth or withhold the moral effort required to resist temptation and rise to duty, is to be found an act which is free in the sense required for moral responsibility; an act of which the self is sole author, and of which it is true that "it could be" (or, after the event, "could have been") "otherwise." Such is the thesis which we shall now try to establish.

The species of argument appropriate to the establishment of a thesis of this sort should fall, I think, into two phases. First, there should be a consideration of the evidence of the moral agent's own inner experience. What *is* the act of moral decision, and what does it imply, from the standpoint of the actual participant? Since there is no way of knowing the act of moral decision—or for that matter any other form of activity—except by actual participation in it, the evidence of the subject, or agent, is on an issue of this kind of palmary importance. It can hardly, however, be taken as in itself conclusive. For even if that evidence should be overwhelmingly to the effect that moral decision does have the characteristics required by moral freedom, the question is bound to be raised—and in view of considerations from other quarters pointing in a contrary direction is *rightly* raised— Can we *trust* the evidence of inner experience? That brings us to what will be the second phase of the argument. We shall have to go on to show, if we are to make good our case, that the extraneous considerations so often supposed to be fatal to the belief in moral freedom are in fact innocuous to it.

In the light of what was said in the last lecture about the self's experience of moral decision as a *creative* activity, we may perhaps be absolved from developing the first phase of the argument at any great length. The appeal is throughout to one's own experience in the actual taking of the moral decision in the situation of moral temptation. "Is it possible," we must ask, "for anyone so circumstanced to *dis*believe that we could be deciding otherwise?" The answer is surely not in doubt. When we decide to exert moral effort to resist a temptation, we feel quite certain that we *could* withhold the effort; just as, if we decide to withhold the effort and yield to our desires, we feel quite certain that we *could* exert it—otherwise we should not blame ourselves afterwards for having succumbed. It may be, indeed, that this conviction is mere self-delusion. But that is not at the moment our concern. It is enough at present to establish that the act of deciding to exert or to withhold moral effort, as we know it from the inside in actual moral living, belongs to the category of acts which "could have been otherwise."

Mutatis mutandis, the same reply is forthcoming if we ask, "Is it possible for the moral agent in the taking of his decision to *dis*believe that he is the *sole* author of that decision?" Clearly he cannot disbelieve that it is *he* who takes the decision. That, however, is not in itself sufficient to enable him, on reflection, to regard himself as *solely* responsible for the act. For his "character" as so far formed might conceivably be a factor in determining it, and no one can suppose the constitution of his "character" is uninfluenced by circumstances of heredity and environment with which *he* has nothing to do. . . . the very essence of the moral decision as it is experienced is that it is a decision whether or not to *combat* our strongest desire, and our strongest desire *is* the expression in the situation of our character as so far formed. Now clearly our character cannot be a factor in determining the decision whether or not to *oppose* our character. I think we are entitled to say, therefore, that the act of moral decision is one in which the self is for itself not merely "author" but "sole author."

We may pass on, then, to the second phase of our constructive argument; and this will demand more elaborate treatment. Even if a moral agent *qua* making a moral decision in the situation of "temptation" cannot help believing that he has free will in the sense at issue—a moral freedom between real alternatives, between genuinely open possibilities—are there, nevertheless, objections to a freedom of this kind so cogent that we are bound to distrust the evidence of "inner experience"?

I begin by drawing attention to a simple point whose significance tends, I think, to be under-estimated. If the phenomenological analysis we have offered is substantially correct, no one while functioning as a moral agent can help believing that he enjoys free will. Theoretically he may be completely convinced by Determinist arguments, but when actually confronted with a personal situation of conflict between duty and desire he is quite certain that it lies with him here and now whether or not he will rise to duty. It follows that if Determinists could produce convincing theoretical arguments against a free will of this kind, the awkward predicament would ensue that man has to deny as a theoretical being what he has to assert as a practical being. Now I think the Determinist ought to be a good deal more worried about this than he usually is. He seems to imagine that a strong case on general theoretical grounds is enough to prove that the "practical" belief in free will, even if inescapable for us as practical beings, is mere illusion. But in fact it proves nothing of the sort. There is no reason whatever why a belief that we find ourselves obliged to hold *qua* practical beings should be required to give way before a belief which we find ourselves obliged to hold *qua* theoretical beings; or, for that matter, *vice versa*. All that the theoretical arguments of Determinism can prove, unless they are reinforced by a refutation of the phenomenological analysis that supports Libertarianism, is that there is a radical conflict between the theoretical and the practical sides of man's nature, an antimony at the very heart of the self. And this is a state of affairs with which no one can easily rest satisfied. I think therefore that the Determinist ought to concern himself a great deal more than he does with phenomenological analysis, in order to show, if he can, that the assurance of free will is not really an inexpugnable element in man's practical consciousness. There is just as much obligation upon him, convinced though he may be of the soundness of his theoretical arguments, to expose the errors of the Libertarian's phenomenological analysis, as there is upon us, convinced though we may be of the soundness of the Libertarian's phenomenological analysis, to expose the errors of the Determinist's theoretical arguments.

However, we must at once begin the discharge of our own obligation. The rest of this lecture will be devoted to trying to show that the arguments which seem to carry most weight with Determinists are, to say the least of it, very far from compulsive.

Fortunately a good many of the arguments which at an earlier time in the history of philosophy would have been strongly urged against us make almost no appeal to the bulk of philosophers today, and we may here pass them by. That applies to any criticism of "open possibilities" based on a metaphysical theory about the nature of the universe as a whole. Nobody today *has* a metaphysical theory about the nature of the universe as a whole! It applies also, with almost equal force, to criticism based upon the universality of causal law as a supposed postulate of science. There have always been, in my opinion, sound philosophic reasons for doubting the validity, as distinct from the convenience, of the causal postulate in its universal form, but at the present time, when scientists themselves are deeply divided about the need for postulating causality even within their own special field, we shall do better to concentrate our attention upon criticisms which are more confidently advanced. I propose to ignore also, on different grounds, the type of criticism of free will that is sometimes advanced from the side of religion, based upon religious postulates of Divine Omnipotence and Omniscience. So far as I can see, a postulate of human freedom is every bit as necessary to meet certain religious demands (*e.g.*, to make sense of the "conviction of sin"), as postulates of Divine Omniscience and Omnipotence are to meet certain other religious demands. If so, then it can hardly be argued that religious experience as such tells more strongly against than for the position we are defending; and we may be satisfied, in the present context, to leave the matter there. It will be more profitable to discuss certain arguments which contemporary philosophers do think important, and which recur with a somewhat monotonous regularity in the literature of anti-Libertarianism.

These arguments can, I think, be reduced in principle to no more than two: first, the argument from "predictability"; second, the argument from the alleged meaninglessness of an act supposed to be the self's act and yet not an expression of the self's character. Contemporary criticism of free will seems to me to consist almost exclusively of variations of these two themes. I shall deal with each in turn.

On the first we touched in passing at an earlier stage. Surely it is beyond question (the critic urges) that when we know a person intimately we can foretell with a high degree of accuracy how he will respond to at least a large number of practical situations. One feels safe in predicting that one's dog-loving friend will not use his boot to repel the little mongrel that comes yapping at his heels; or again that one's wife will not pass with incurious eyes (or indeed pass at all) the new hat shop in the city. So to behave would not be (as we say) "in character." But, so the criticism runs, you with your doctrine of "genuinely open possibilities," of a free will by which the self can diverge from its own character, remove all rational basis from such prediction. You require us to make the absurd supposition that the success of countless predictions of the sort in the past has been mere matter of chance. If you *really* believed in your theory, you would not be surprised if tomorrow your friend with the notorious horror of strong drink should suddenly exhibit a passion for whisky and soda, or if your friend whose taste for reading has hitherto been satisfied with the sporting columns of the newspapers should be discovered on a fine Saturday afternoon poring over the works of Hegel. But of course you *would* be surprised. Social life would be sheer chaos if there were not well-grounded social expectations; and social life is not sheer chaos. Your theory is hopelessly wrecked upon obvious facts.

Now whether or not this criticism holds good against some versions of Libertarian theory I need not here discuss. It is sufficient if I can make it clear that against the version advanced in this lecture, according to which free will is localised in a relatively narrow field of operation, the criticism has no relevance whatsoever.

Let us remind ourselves briefly of the setting within which, on our view, free will functions. There is X, the course which we believe we ought to follow, and Y, the course towards which we feel our desire is strongest. The freedom which we ascribe to the agent is the freedom to put forth or refrain from putting forth the moral effort required to resist the pressure of desire and do what he thinks he ought to do.

But then there is surely an immense range of practical situations— covering by far the greater part of life—in which there is no question of a conflict within the self between what he most desires to do and what he thinks he ought to do. Indeed such conflict is a comparatively rare phenomenon for the majority of men. Yet over that whole vast range there is nothing whatever in our version of Libertarianism to prevent our agreeing that character determines conduct. In the absence, real or supposed, of any "moral" issue, what a man chooses will be simply that course which, after such reflection as seems called for, he deems most likely to bring him what he most strongly desires; and that is the same as to say the course to which his present character inclines him.

Over by far the greater area of human choices, then, our theory offers no more barrier to successful prediction on the basis of character than any other theory. For where there is no clash of strongest desire with duty, the free will we are defending has no business. There is just nothing for it to do.

But what about the situations—rare enough though they may be —in which there *is* this clash and in which free will does therefore operate? Does our theory entail that there at any rate, as the critic seems to suppose, "anything may happen"?

Not by any manner of means. In the first place, and by the very nature of the case, the range of the agent's possible choices is bounded by what he thinks he ought to do on the one hand, and what he most strongly desires on the other. The freedom claimed for him is a freedom of decision to make or withhold the effort required to do what he thinks he ought to do. There is no question of a freedom to act in some "wild" fashion, out of all relation to his characteristic beliefs and desires. This so-called "freedom of caprice," so often charged against the Libertarian, is, to put it bluntly, a sheer figment of the critic's imagination, with no *habitat* in serious Libertarian theory. Even in situations where free will does come into play it is perfectly possible, on a view like ours, given the appropriate knowledge of a man's character, to predict within certain limits how he will respond.

But "probable" prediction in such situations can, I think, go further than this. It is obvious that where desire and duty are at odds, the felt "gap" (as it were) between the two may vary enormously in breadth in different cases. The moderate drinker and the chronic tippler may each want another glass, and each deem it his duty to abstain, but the felt gap between desire and duty in the case of the former is trivial beside the great gulf which is felt to separate them in the case of the latter. Hence it will take a far harder moral effort for the tippler than for the moderate drinker to achieve the same external result of abstention. So much is matter of common agreement. And we are entitled, I think, to take it into account in prediction, on the simple principle that the harder the moral effort required to resist desire the less likely it is to occur. Thus in the example taken, most people would predict that the tippler will very probably succumb to his desires, whereas there is a reasonable likelihood that the moderate drinker will make the comparatively slight effort needed to resist them. So long as the prediction does not pretend to more than a measure of probability, there is nothing in our theory which would disallow it.

I claim, therefore, that the view of free will I have been putting forward is consistent with predictability of conduct on the basis of character over a very wide field indeed. And I make the further claim that the field will cover all the situations in life concerning which there is any empirical evidence that successful prediction is possible.

Let us pass on to consider the second main line of criticism. This is, I think, much the more illuminating of the two, if only because it compels the Libertarian to make explicit certain concepts which are indispensable to him, but which, being desperately hard to state clearly, are apt not to be stated at all. The critic's fundamental point might be stated somewhat as follows:

"Free will as you describe it is completely unintelligible. On your own showing no *reason* can be given, because there just *is* no reason, why a man decides to exert rather than to withhold moral effort, or *vice versa*. But such an act—or more properly, such an 'occurrence' —it is nonsense to speak of as an act of a *self*. If there is nothing in the self's character to which it is, even in principle, in any way trace-able, the self has nothing to do with it. Your so-called 'freedom,' therefore, so far from supporting the self's moral responsibility, destroys it as surely as the crudest Determinism could do."

If we are to discuss this criticism usefully, it is important, I think, to begin by getting clear about two different senses of the word "intelligible."

If, in the first place, we mean by an "intelligible" act one whose occurrence is in principle capable of being inferred, since it follows necessarily from something (though we may not know in fact from what), then it is certainly true that the Libertarian's free will is un-intelligible. But that is only saying, is it not, that the Libertarian's "free" act is not an act which follows necessarily from something! This can hardly rank as a *criticism* of Libertarianism. It is just a description of it. That there can be nothing unintelligible in *this* sense is precisely what the Determinist has got to *prove*.

Yet it is surprising how often the critic of Libertarianism involves himself in this circular mode of argument. Repeatedly it is urged against the Libertarian, with a great air of triumph, that on his view he can't say *why* I now decide to rise to duty, or now decide to follow my strongest desire in defiance of duty. Of course he can't. If he could he wouldn't *be* a Libertarian. To "account for" a "free" act is a contradiction in terms. A free will is *ex hypothesi* the sort of thing of which the request for an *explanation* is absurd. The assumption that an explanation must be in principle possible for the act of moral decision deserves to rank as a classic example of the ancient fallacy of "begging the question."

But the critic usually has in mind another sense of the word "un-intelligible." He is apt to take it for granted that an act which is unintelligible in the *above* sense (as the morally free act of the Lib-ertarian undoubtedly is) is unintelligible in the *further* sense that we can attach no meaning to it. And this is an altogether more serious matter. If it could really be shown that the Libertarian's "free will" were unintelligible in this sense of being meaningless, that, for myself at any rate, would be the end of the affair. Libertarianism would have been conclusively refuted.

But it seems to me manifest that this can *not* be shown. The critic has allowed himself, I submit, to become the victim of a widely accepted but fundamentally vicious assumption. He has assumed that whatever is meaningful must exhibit its meaningfulness to those who view it from the standpoint of external observation. Now if one chooses thus to limit one's self to the rôle of external observer, it is, I think, perfectly true that one can attach no meaning to an act which is the act of something we call a "self" and yet follows from nothing in that self's character. But then *why should we* so limit ourselves, when what is under consideration is a subjective activity? For the apprehension of subjective acts there is *another* standpoint available, that of *inner experience,* of the practical consciousness in its actual functioning. If our free will should turn out to be something to which we can attach a meaning from this standpoint, no more is required. And no more ought to be expected. For I must repeat that only from the inner standpoint of living experience *could* anything of the nature of "activity" be directly grasped. Observation from without is in the nature of the case impotent to apprehend the active *qua* active. We can from without observe sequences of states. If into these we read activity (as we sometimes do), this can only be on the basis of what we discern in ourselves from the inner standpoint. It follows that if anyone insists upon taking his criterion of the meaningful simply from the standpoint of external observation, he is really deciding in advance of the evidence that the notion of activity, and *a fortiori* the notion of a free will, is "meaningless." He looks for the free act through a medium which is in the nature of the case incapable of revealing it, and then, because inevitably he doesn't find it, he declares that it doesn't exist!

But if, as we surely ought in this context, we adopt the inner standpoint, then (I am suggesting) things appear in a totally different light. From the inner standpoint, it seems to me plain, there is no difficulty whatever in attaching meaning to an act which is the self's act and which nevertheless does not follow from the self's character. So much I claim has been established by the phenomenological analysis, in this . . . lecture, of the act of moral decision in face of moral temptation. It is thrown into particularly clear relief where the moral decision is to make the moral effort required to rise to duty. For the very function of moral effort, as it appears to the agent engaged in the act, is to enable the self to act against the line of least resistance, against the line to which his character as so far formed most strongly inclines him. But if the self is thus conscious here of *combating* his formed character, he surely cannot possibly suppose that the act, although his own act, *issues from* his formed character? I submit, therefore, that the self knows very well indeed —from the inner standpoint—what is meant by an act which is the *self's* act and which nevertheless does not follow from the self's *character*.

What this implies—and it seems to me to be an implication of cardinal importance for any theory of the self that aims at being more than superficial—is that the nature of the self is for itself something more than just its character as so far formed. The "nature" of the self and what we commonly call the "character" of the self are by no means the same thing, and it is utterly vital that they should not be confused. The "nature" of the self comprehends, but is not without remainder reducible to, its "character"; it must, if we are to be true to the testimony of our experience of it, be taken as including *also* the authentic creative power of fashioning and re-fashioning "character."

The misguided, and as a rule quite uncritical, belittlement, of the evidence offered by inner experience has, I am convinced, been responsible for more bad argument by the opponents of Free Will than has any other single factor. How often, for example, do we find the Determinist critic saying, in effect, "*Either* the act follows necessarily upon precedent states, *or* it is a mere matter of chance and accordingly of no moral significance." The disjunction is invalid, for it does not exhaust the possible alternatives. It seems to the critic to do so only because he *will* limit himself to the standpoint which is proper, and indeed alone possible, in dealing with the physical world, the standpoint of the external observer. If only he would allow himself to assume the standpoint which is not merely proper for, but necessary to, the apprehension of subjective activity, the inner standpoint of the practical consciousness in its actual functioning, he would find himself obliged to recognise the falsity of his disjunction. Reflection upon the act of moral decision as apprehended from the inner standpoint would force him to recognise a *third* possibility, as remote from chance as from necessity, that, namely, of *creative activity,* in which (as I have ventured to express it) nothing determines the act save the agent's doing of it.

There we must leave the matter. But as this lecture has been, I know, somewhat densely packed, it may be helpful if I conclude by reminding you, in bald summary, of the main things I have been trying to say. Let me set them out in so many successive theses.

(1) The freedom which is at issue in the traditional Free Will problem is the freedom which is presupposed in moral responsibility.

(2) Critical reflection upon carefully considered attributions of moral responsibility reveals that the only freedom that will do is a freedom which pertains to inner acts of choice, and that these acts must be acts (a) of which the self is *sole* author, and (b) which the self could have performed otherwise.

(3) From phenomenological analysis of the situation of moral temptation we find that the self as engaged in this situation is inescapably convinced that it possesses a freedom of precisely the specified kind, located in the decision to exert or withhold the moral effort needed to rise to duty where the pressure of its desiring nature is felt to urge it in a contrary direction.

Passing to the question of the *reality* of this moral freedom which the moral agent believes himself to possess, we argued:

(4) Of the two types of Determinist criticism which seem to have most influence today, that based on the predictability of much human behaviour fails to touch a Libertarianism which confines the area of free will as above indicated. Libertarianism so understood is compatible with all the predictability that the empirical facts warrant. And:

(5) The second main type of criticisms, which alleges the "meaninglessness" of an act which is the self's act and which is yet not determined by the self's character, is based on a failure to appreciate that the standpoint of inner experience is not only legitimate but indispensable where what is at issue is the reality and nature of a subjective activity. The creative act of moral decision is inevitably meaningless to the mere external observer; but from the inner standpoint it is as real, and as significant, as anything in human experience.

LORENZO DE VALLA

Dialogue on Free Will

Lorenzo. What do you ask me to explain to you?

Antonio. Whether the foreknowledge of God stands in the way of free will and whether Boethius has correctly argued this question.

Lor. I shall attend to Boethius later; but if I satisfy you in this matter, I want you to make a promise.

Ant. What sort of a promise?

Lor. That if I serve you splendidly in this luncheon, you will not want to be entertained again for dinner.

Ant. What do you mean as lunch for me and what as dinner, for I do not understand?

Lor. That contented after discussing this one question, you will not ask for another afterward.

Ant. You say another? As if this one will not be sufficient and more! I freely promise that I will ask no dinner from you.

Lor. Go ahead then and get into the very heart of the question.

Ant. You advise well. If God foresees the future, it cannot happen otherwise than He foresaw. For example, if He sees that Judas will be a traitor, it is impossible for him not to become a traitor, that is, it is necessary for Judas to betray, unless—which should be far from us—we assume God to lack providence. Since He has providence, one must undoubtedly believe that mankind does not have free will in its own power; and I do not speak particularly of evil men, for as it is necessary for these to do evil, so conversely it is necessary for the good to do good, provided those are still to be called good or evil who lack will or that their actions are to be con-

---

* From Cassirer, Kristeller, and Randall, eds., *The Renaissance Philosophy of Man* (Chicago, Ill.: University of Chicago Press, 1948), pp. 161–71. Reprinted by permission of the editors and the publishers.

111

sidered right or wrong which are necessary and forced. And what now follows you yourself see: for God either to praise this one for justice or accuse that of injustice and to reward the one and punish the other, to speak freely, seems to be the opposite of justice, since the actions of men follow by necessity the foreknowledge of God. We should therefore abandon religion, piety, sanctity, ceremonies, sacrifices; we may expect nothing from Him, employ no prayers, not call upon his mercy at all, neglect to improve our mind, and, finally, do nothing except what pleases us, since our justice or injustice is foreknown by God. Consequently, it seems that either He does not foresee the future if we are endowed with will or He is not just if we lack free will. There you have what makes me inclined to doubt in this matter.

Lor. You have indeed not only pushed into the middle of the question but have even more widely extended it. You say God foresaw that Judas would be a traitor, but did He on that account induce him to betrayal? I do not see that, for, although God may foreknow some future act to be done by man, this act is not done by necessity because he may do it willingly. Moreover, what is voluntary cannot be necessary.

Ant. Do not expect me to give in to you so easily or to flee without sweat and blood.

Lor. Good luck to you; let us contend closely in hand-to-hand and foot-to-foot conflict. Let the decision be by sword, not spear.

Ant. You say Judas acted voluntarily and on that account not by necessity. Indeed, it would be most shameless to deny that he did it voluntarily. What do I say to that? Certainly this act of will was necessary since God foreknew it; moreover, since it was foreknown by Him, it was necessary for Judas to will and do it lest he should make the foreknowledge in any way false.

Lor. Still I do not see why the necessity for our volitions and actions should derive from God's foreknowledge. For, if foreknowing something *will be* makes it come about, surely knowing something *is* just as easily makes the same thing *be*. Certainly, if I know your genius, you would not say that something *is* because you *know* it is. For example, you know it is now day; because you know it is, is it on that account also day? Or, conversely, because it is day, do you for that reason know it is day?

Ant. Indeed, continue.

Lor. The same reasoning applies to the past. I know it was night eight hours ago, but my knowledge does not make that it was night; rather I know it was night because it was night. Again, that I may come closer to the point, I know in advance that after eight hours it will be night; and will it be on that account? Not at all, because it will be night, for that reason I foreknew it; now if the foreknowledge of man is not the cause of something occurring, neither is the foreknowledge of God.

Ant. Believe me, that comparison deceives us; it is one thing to know the present and past, another to know the future. For when I know something is, it cannot be changed, as that day, which now is, cannot be made not to be. Also the past does not differ from the present, for we did not notice the day when it was past but while it was occurring as the present; I learned it was night not then when it *had passed* but when it was. And so for these times I concede that something *was,* or *is,* not because I know it but that I know it because it *is* or *was.* But a different reasoning applies to the future because it is subject to change. It cannot be known for certain because it is uncertain. And, in order that we may not defraud God of foreknowledge, we must admit that the future is certain and on that account necessary; this is what deprives us of free will. Nor can you say what you said just now that the future is not preordained merely because God foresees it but that God foresees it because the future is preordained; you thus wound God by implying that it is necessary for him to foreknow the future.

Lor. You have come well armed and weaponed for the fight, but let us see who is deceived, you or I. First, however, I would meet this latter point where you say that, if God foresees the future because it is to be, He labors under the necessity to foresee the future. Indeed this should not be attributed to necessity but to nature, to will, to power, unless it is an attribute of weakness perchance that God cannot sin, cannot die, cannot give up His wisdom rather than an attribute of power and of divinity. Thus, when we said He is unable to escape foresight, which is a form of wisdom, we inflicted no wound on Him but did Him honor. So I shall not be afraid to say that God is unable to escape foreseeing what is to be. I come now to your first point: that the present and the past are unalterable and therefore knowable; that the future is alterable and therefore not capable of being foreknown. I ask if it can be changed that at eight hours from now night will arrive, that after summer there will be autumn, after autumn winter, after winter spring, after spring summer?

Ant. Those are natural phenomena always running the same course; I speak, however, of matters of the will.

Lor. What do you say of chance things? Can they be foreseen by God without necessity being imputed to them? Perchance today it may rain or I may find a treasure, would you concede this could be foreknown without any necessity?

Ant. Why should I not concede it? Do you believe I think so ill of God?

Lor. Make sure that you do not think ill when you say you think well. For if you concede in this case, why should you doubt in matters of the will, for both classes of events can happen in two different ways?

Ant. The matter is not that way. For these chance things follow a certain nature of their own, and for this reason doctors, sailors, and farmers are accustomed to foresee much, since they reckon consequences out of antecedents, which cannot happen in affairs of the will. Predict which foot I will move first, and, whichever you have said, you will lie, since I shall move the other.

Lor. I ask you, who was ever found so clever as this Glarea? He thinks he can impose on God like the man in Aesop who consulted Apollo whether the sparrow he held under his coat was dead for the sake of deceiving him. For you have not told me to predict, but God. Indeed, I have not the ability to predict whether there will be a good vintage, such as you ascribe to farmers. But by saying and also believing that God does not know which foot you will move first, you involve yourself in great sin.

Ant. Do you think I affirm something rather than raise the question for the sake of the argument? Again you seem to seek excuses by your speech and, giving ground, decline to fight.

Lor. As if I fought for the sake of victory rather than truth! Witness how I am driven from my ground; do you grant that God now knows your will even better than you yourself do?

Ant. I indeed grant it.

Lor. It is also necessary that you grant that you will do nothing other than the will decides.

Ant. Of course.

Lor. How then can He not know the action if He knows the will which is the source of the action?

Ant. Not at all, for I myself do not know what I shall do even though I know what I have in my will. For I do not will to move this foot or that foot, in any case, but the other than He will have announced. And so, if you compare me with God, just as I do not know what I will do, so He does not know.

Lor. What difficulty is there in meeting this sophism of yours? He knows that you are prepared to reply otherwise than He will say and that you will move the left first if the right is named by Him; whichever one He should say therefore, it is certain to Him what will happen.

Ant. Yet which of the two will He say?

Lor. Do you speak of God? Let me know your will and I will announce what will happen.

Ant. Go ahead, you try to know my will.

Lor. You will move the right one first.

Ant. Behold, the left one.

Lor. How have you shown my foreknowledge to be false, since I knew you would move the left one?

Ant. But why did you say other than you thought?

Lor. In order to deceive you by your own arts and to deceive the man willing to deceive.

Ant. But God Himself would not lie nor deceive in replying, nor did you do rightly in replying for Another as He would not reply.

Lor. Did you not tell me to "predict"? Therefore, I should not speak for God but for myself whom you asked.

Ant. How changeable you are. A little while ago you were saying I told God to "predict," not you; now on the contrary you say the opposite. Let God reply which foot I will move first.

Lor. How ridiculous, as if He would answer you!

Ant. What? Can He not indeed reply truly if He wishes?

Lor. Rather He can lie who is the Truth itself.

Ant. What would He reply then?

Lor. Certainly what you will do, but, you not hearing, He might say to me, He might say to one of those other people, He might say it to many; and, when He has done that, do you not think He will truly have predicted?

Ant. Yea, indeed, He will have truly predicted, but what would you think if He predicted it to me?

Lor. Believe me, you who thus lie in wait to deceive God, if you should hear or certainly know what He said you would do, either out of love or out of fear you would hasten to do what you knew was predicted by Him. But let us skip this which has nothing to do with foreknowledge. For it is one thing to foreknow and another to predict the future. Say whatever you have in mind about foreknowledge, but leave prediction out of it.

Ant. So be it, for the things that I have said were spoken not so much for me as against you. I return from this digression to where I said it was necessary for Judas to betray, unless we entirely annul providence, because God foresaw it would be thus. So if it was possible for something to happen otherwise than it was foreseen, providence is destroyed; but if it is impossible, free will is destroyed, a thing no less unworthy to God than if we should cancel His providence. I, in what concerns me, would prefer Him to be less wise rather than less good. The latter would injure mankind; the other would not.

Lor. I praise your modesty and wisdom. When you are not able to win, you do not fight on stubbornly but give in and apply yourself to another defense, which seems to be the argument of what you set forth a while back. In reply to this argument, I deny that foreknowledge can be deceived as the consequence of the possibility that something might turn out otherwise than as it has been foreseen. For what prevents it from also being true that something can turn out otherwise than it will immediately happen? Something that can happen and something that will happen are very different. I can be a husband, I can be a soldier or a priest, but will I right away? Not at all. Though I can do otherwise than will happen, nevertheless I shall not do otherwise; and it was in Judas' power not to sin even though it was foreseen that he would, but he preferred to sin, which it was foreseen would happen. Thus foreknowledge is valid and free will abides. This will make a choice between two alternatives, for to do both is not possible, and He foreknows by His own light which will be chosen.

Ant. Here I have you. Are you unaware of the philosophical rule that whatever is possible ought to be conceded as if it were? It is possible for something to happen otherwise than it is foreknown; it may be granted it will happen that way, through which it is now manifest that foreknowledge is deceived since it happens otherwise than foreknowledge had believed.

Lor. Are you using formulas of philosophers on me? Indeed, as if I would not dare to contradict them! Certainly I think that precept you mention, whose ever it is, most absurd, for I can concede it to be possible to move the right foot first, and we may concede it will be so, and I can also concede it possible for me to move the left foot first, and we may concede this will be as well; I will move therefore both the left before the right and the right before the left, and through your concession of the possible I arrive at the impossible. Therefore, know that it is not to be conceded that whatever is possible will likewise happen. It is possible for you to do otherwise than God foreknows, nevertheless you will not do otherwise, nor will you therefore deceive Him.

Ant. I will not object further, nor, since I smashed all my weapons, will I fight with tooth and nail as is said; but, if there is any other point through which you can explain it to me more amply and plainly persuade, I wish to hear it.

Lor. You covet the praise of wisdom and modesty again, since you are your true self. And so I will do as you ask because I was doing it anyway of my own will. For what has been said so far is not what I had decided to say but what need of defense itself demanded. Now attend to what persuades me and perhaps it will even persuade you that foreknowledge is no impediment to free will. However, would you prefer me to touch on this subject briefly or to explain it more clearly at greater length?

Ant. It always seems to me, indeed, that those who speak lucidly speak most briefly, while those who speak obscurely, though in the fewest words, are always more lengthy. Besides, fulness of expression has itself a certain appropriateness and aptness for persuasion. Wherefore, since I asked you from the start that this matter be more lucidly stated by you, you should not doubt my wishes; nevertheless, do whatever is more agreeable to you. For I would never put my judgment ahead of yours.

Lor. Indeed, it is of importance to me to follow your wish, and whatever you think more convenient I do also. Apollo, who was so greatly celebrated among the Greeks, either through his own nature or by concession of the other gods, had foresight and knowledge of all future things, not only those which pertained to men but to the gods as well; thus, if we may believe the tradition, and nothing prevents our accepting it just for the moment, Apollo rendered true and certain prophecies about those consulting him. Sextus Tarquinius consulted him as to what would happen to himself. We may pretend that he replied, as was customary, in verse as follows:

> An exile and a pauper you will fall,
> Killed by the angry city.

To this Sextus: "What are you saying, Apollo? Have I deserved thus of you that you announce me a fate so cruel, that you assign me such a sad condition of death? Repeal your response, I implore you, predict happier things; you should be better disposed toward me who so royally endowed you." In reply Apollo: "Your gifts, O youth, certainly are agreeable and acceptable to me; in return for which I have rendered a miserable and sad prophecy; I wish it were happier, but it is not in my power to do this. I know the fates, I do not decide them; I am able to announce Fortune, not change her; I am the index of destinies, not the arbiter; I would reveal better things if better things awaited. Certainly this is not my fault who cannot prevent even my own misfortune that I foresee. Accuse Jupiter, if you will, accuse the fates, accuse Fortune whence the course of events descends. The power and decision over the fates are seated with them; with me, mere foreknowledge and prediction. You earnestly besought an oracle; I gave it. You inquired after the truth; I was unable to tell a lie. You have come to my temple from a far-distant region, and I ought not to send you away without a reply. Two things are most alien to me: falsehood and silence." Could Sextus justly reply to this speech: "Yea, indeed, it is your fault, Apollo, who foresee my fate with your wisdom, for, unless you had foreseen it, this would not be about to happen to me"?

Ant. Not only would he speak unjustly but he should never reply thus.

Lor. How then?

Ant. Why do you not say?

Lor. Should he not reply in this way: "Indeed, I give thanks to you, holy Apollo, who have neither deceived me with falsehood nor spurned me in silence. But this also I ask you to tell me: Why is Jupiter so unjust, so cruel, that he should assign such a sad fate to me, an undeserving, innocent worshiper of the gods"?

Ant. Certainly I would reply in this way if I were Sextus, but what did Apollo reply to him?

Lor. "You call yourself undeserving and innocent, Sextus? You may be sure that the crimes that you will commit, the adulteries, betrayals, perjuries, the almost hereditary arrogance are to blame." Would Sextus then reply this way: "The fault for my crimes must rather be assigned to you, for it is necessary for me, who you foreknow will sin, to sin"?

Ant. Sextus would be mad as well as unjust if he replied in that way.

Lor. Do you have anything that you might say on his behalf?

Ant. Absolutely nothing.

Lor. If therefore Sextus had nothing which could be argued against the foreknowledge of Apollo, certainly Judas had nothing either which might accuse the foreknowledge of God. And, if that is so, certainly the question by which you said you were confused and disturbed is answered.

· ·

CARL GINET

Can the Will be Caused?

Two views of the problem about freedom of the will that occur frequently in philosophical literature, and elsewhere, can be stated in terms of their questions about the two propositions: (I) The will is caused. (II) The will is free.[1]

One view naïvely assumes that these propositions are logical contradictories and that there is no important difficulty about the meaning of either. It simply raises the question: Which is true? A familiar argument for (II) is based on an appeal to introspective evidence that (I) is false. The case against (II) is often argued by claiming that science requires (or confirms) a general deterministic postulate that entails (I) or by supporting (I) directly with talk of how a person's past determines his motives and his motives determine his voluntary acts.

Another, I think more penetrating, view takes as fundamental the question whether the two propositions are indeed logically incompatible. Most philosophers raising this question have (through suitable explications of what "free" means) answered it negatively.[2] This

* From Carl Ginet, "Can the Will be Caused?" *The Philosophical Review*, LXXI (1962), 49–55. Reprinted by permission of the editors and the author.

[1] I should like to acknowledge my indebtedness to Professor John Rawls, who gave me the initial suggestion for the argument of this paper and help with its development. None of the thoughts here, however, should be attributed to him.

[2] For example: Hobbes, Hume, Mill, Moore, Schlick, Nowell-Smith. Some have argued that (I) and (II) *are* logically incompatible on the basis of their own examination of the senses of the predicates involved. See, for example, C. D. Broad,

is not surprising because the question has nearly always been prompted by the feeling that there are good reasons for accepting both propositions: (I) seems to be supported by the common practice of explaining choices, decisions, volitions, as due to certain psychological attributes of the agent (his desires, beliefs, and the like); (II) seems to be supported by the common practice of appraising choices and agents' reasons for them and of holding agents responsible for them, in which it is assumed that the agents could have chosen otherwise.

Although this second approach to the problem does question one assumption of the more naïve approach, it overlooks another important point. For it still shares with the naïve view the assumption that both (I) and (II) are meaningful descriptions of possible states of affairs. Challenging this assumption in the case of (I) should lead to a better understanding of the problem. To this end I shall argue that (I) is *necessarily* false, that it is conceptually impossible that the will should be caused. The idea that it can be caused is a philosophical mistake, based on notions that cannot be reconciled with our actual concept of deciding.

I take it that (I) can, without argument, be translated to read: All volitions, choices, and decisions are caused. Thus to argue that (I) is not conceptually possible it will suffice to argue that it is not conceptually possible that a decision should be caused.

This conclusion follows directly from the following two propositions:

(A) It is conceptually impossible for a person to know what a decision of his is going to be before he makes it.

(B) If it were conceptually possible for a decision to be caused, then it would be conceptually possible for a person to know what a decision of his was going to be before making it.

I shall argue for each of these separately.

"Determinism, Indeterminism, and Libertarianism," in *Ethics and the History of Philosophy* (New York, 1952), esp. pp. 201–11; and C. A. Campbell, "Is 'Free Will' a Pseudo-Problem?" *Mind*, LX (1951), 441–65.

(A): This proposition goes counter to the thinking of some acute philosophers,[3] but the following considerations should make it convincing.

No one can be intelligibly described as knowing what his decision will be before he makes it because the claim to possess such knowledge is implicitly inconsistent. One may be prevented from seeing this, however, by the fact that certain utterances *appear* to make such a claim and yet are susceptible of intelligible interpretation.

For example, consider an utterance of the form "I know now that I shall later decide to do. . . ." There is more than one thing a person might mean by such a remark: he might mean that he has made his decision as to what he will do and so knows what decision he will later announce; or he might mean that he has made his decision as to what he will do and so knows what decision he will later pretend to make; or he might mean that he has made his decision but thinks he will later forget his present intention and make the same decision again. But his meaning anything at all by it depends on the fact that the locution "I know now that I shall later . . ." is commonly used to *express* a present decision concerning future action. Any attempt to understand the remark above must rely on this fact and regard the remark, not as a claim to know what a decision not yet made will be, but as the expression of a decision already made about future action.

The remark must be so regarded because any expansion explicitly denying that the speaker was making this decision-expressing use of "I know that I shall later . . ." also reduces it to absurdity. Consider. "I already know (am quite certain) that I shall later decide to do . . . , but I have not yet decided what I shall do, that is, I've not yet made up my mind what I shall do, that is, I do not yet know what I shall do." Now this utterance clearly makes two *inconsistent* claims: on the one hand, that the speaker knows what he will decide to do, hence, what he will at least try to do; on the other hand, that he does *not* know what he will try to do.

[3] For example, Bertrand Russell in *Our Knowledge of the External World* (Chicago, 1929), pp. 254–55, imagines "a set of beings who know the whole future with absolute certainty," who "would not have to wait for the event in order to know what decision they were going to adopt on some future occasion," and says that they would not regret this knowledge because "human actions are the outcome of desire, and no foreseeing can be true unless it takes account of desire."

For a person to claim that he knows what he will decide to do, hence, what he will at least try to do, and *then* to begin the process of making up his mind what he will do—trying to persuade himself one way or another by offering himself reasons for and against the various alternatives—would surely be a procedure of which we could make no sense. Either his undertaking to make a decision belies his prior claim to knowledge, or his prior claim makes a farce of his undertaking to make a decision. If he does already know what he will decide to do, then he cannot by the process of making up his mind persuade himself of anything that he does not already know. Yet the whole point of making up one's mind is to pass from uncertainty to a kind of knowledge about what one will do or try to do. To believe that someone already knows what his future attempted action will be is to refuse to regard anything he does as having the point necessary to its being his *deciding* that he will attempt the action. (Analogously, if someone knows already how the pieces of a puzzle go together to form a required shape, then nothing he might do, while knowing that, can count as his *figuring out* how the pieces go together to form the required shape.)

Thus it is unintelligible to describe someone as undertaking to make up his mind and as *knowing* prior to this undertaking what the outcome of it will be. In other words, the concept of a decision does not allow the possibility of a person's knowing what his decision will be before he makes it.[4]

(B) I shall try to reduce to absurdity just one of several interpretations that might be given to the proposition that decisions are

[4] Some of the conceptual truths on which the argument above relies have been stated by Stuart Hampshire and H. L. A. Hart, "Decision, Intention, and Certainty," *Mind*, LXVII (1958), 1–12. They say (pp. 2–3): " 'He has not yet decided what he will do' entails 'He does not yet know what he will do.' . . . If a man does claim to be able to predict with certainty his own future actions, basing his prediction on induction, then he is implying that the actions in question will be in some sense, or to some degree, involuntary. . . . If it is up to him to decide what he is going to do, then he must still be uncertain what he will do until he has made a decision or until his intentions are formed. . . . The certainty comes at the moment of decision, and indeed constitutes the decision, when the certainty is arrived at in this way, as a result of considering reasons, and not as a result of considering evidence."

caused. This particular interpretation is important because it is one common to many philosophical discussions of the free will problem.

To think of a decision as *caused* (in the sense that interests me here) is to think of a decision as a specific, discriminable event whose occurrence is ascertainable independently of inquiry as to how it was caused, and to think of its being caused as consisting in the fact that there is a set of events and circumstances preceding and accompanying it to which it has a certain relation—the causal relation. This relation is understood to be defined for an indefinite variety of events and circumstances—including even physical events remote from human influence—and, hence, it is in its conception quite independent of any peculiar kinds of events and circumstances that might stand in such relation to each other. It applies just as well to decisions and desires as to explosions and temperatures. This view of the causal relation is Humean to the extent that the relation holds between a particular event A and a certain set of its antecedents B only if it is a true generalization that an event of the same kind as A will always accompany the occurrence of a set of circumstances sufficiently similar to B.

With this interpretation (as far as it goes), if (I) does describe a possible state of affairs then it must be at least logically possible that someone should know what a decision of his will be before he makes it. For if this interpretation did make sense and a decision were caused, then the decider would know his decision in advance if both the following conditions were satisfied: (1) The decider knew prior to his decision the causal law that circumstances of the kind that were going to cause it are always accompanied by a decision of that kind. (2) The decider knew prior to his decision that circumstances of the required kind existed or would exist. Under these conditions, the decider would watch a series of causally connected events and circumstances produce a decision of his, knowing all the time what decision would be produced.

The common interpretation of "decisions are caused" that was explained above excludes all grounds from which one might deduce the conceptual impossibility of such a situation. How could the possibility of the first condition be excluded? If a completely universal proposition can be known by anyone then it can be known by everyone; and surely there is no sense in the idea of a true causal law that could not be known by anyone.

How could the possibility of the second condition (that the decider knows prior to his decision of the existence of its causal circumstances) be excluded? One can, of course, describe a set of circumstances that it would be logically impossible for the decider to know in advance of his decision. (One need only include in the set the circumstance that the decider remains ignorant of certain other circumstances in the set at least until the time of the decision. It might be imagined, for example, that an agent's having a certain set of desires, beliefs, perceptions, and attitudes was always sufficient to produce a certain decision provided also that the agent was not aware at the time of some of those attitudes.) And a set of circumstances would not be a less plausible candidate for the cause of a decision merely because it had this feature. But neither could a set of circumstances be ruled out as a candidate for the cause merely because it *lacked* this feature.

Part of the idea being considered is that the notion of the causal relation is a perfectly general one, applicable to all kinds of events, physical and mental. And this surely means that the notion of the causal relation, whatever it does include, cannot include grounds for deducing that in the special case of a decision it is impossible that any set of its circumstances should both have the causal relation to it and be knowable by the decider in advance. Thus we cannot appeal to the meaning of "are caused" in the proposition "decisions are caused" to rule out the embarrassing situation outlined above.

The other part of the idea important to this consideration is that a decision is a specific event which, like a flash or a bang, can be identified independently of inquiry into its causes. It is not supposed that one needs to know what causal law an event falls under before one can identify it is a decision. Rather, as with other kinds of events, the knowledge that one is inquiring about a decision is supposed to guide the causal inquiry, to tell one what sort of causal circumstance to look for, *not* to await the outcome of the inquiry. The meaning of "decisions" proves then to be of no more face-saving value than that of "are caused."

And thus this common interpretation of the proposition that decisions might be caused leaves just as much logical room for the discovery that the set of circumstances to which a decision has the causal relation is one that the decider *could* have known in advance as it does for the discovery that it is not.

In short, if the concept of a decision *were* such that one could ascertain that an event fell under it and then independently ascertain that that event had the causal relation to a certain set of its circumstances, then the concept of a decision *would* allow one to think of (1), (2), and hence, of someone's knowing what his decision will be before he makes it, as genuine possibilities. But in section (*A*) we saw the absurdity of admitting this latter possibility. I conclude that the concept of a decision makes it impossible that any event be both identified as a decision and said to be caused; and, therefore, that proposition (I) is necessarily false.

Two comments should be made on the import of this argument: If we accept the conclusion that (1) is necessarily false we must be prepared to say one of two things about the explanations that we commonly offer for our own and others' decisions—explanations that certainly seem to be in terms of events or circumstances preceding and accompanying those decisions (desires, beliefs, and the like). Either we must say that these explanations are all, not merely false, but guilty of conceptual absurdity in implying that decisions are caused; or we must say that they do not imply that decisions are caused but are explanations of a quite different kind, involving a relation quite different in conception from the causal relation defined in the Humean way. I choose the latter alternative but shall not elaborate it here.

From my argument it does not follow that there are decisions (or choices or volitions). I have shown only that *if* there are decisions, they are (necessarily) not part of the causal order, that explanations of them must be of a different kind. The argument above only removes another of the confusions obscuring the free-will-determinism problem. The real question, it seems to me, is whether a vast addition to our knowledge about the *physical* causes and effects of the minuter internal processes of our bodies could possibly turn out to be incompatible with regarding any of the behavior of those bodies as expressing wills (decisions, choices, volitions). If the answer to this is yes (and there are considerations that can incline one to think it is), then it is an unsettled empirical question whether wills (necessarily free) are attributable to human organisms at all.

part three

RELATIONSHIPS BETWEEN DETERMINISM, FREE WILL AND MORAL RESPONSIBILITY

G. E. MOORE

Free Will

. . . And the very last objection which we considered was one which consisted in asserting that the question whether an action is right or wrong does *not* depend upon its *actual* consequences, because whenever the consequences, *so far as the agent can foresee,* are *likely* to be the best possible, the action is always right, even if they are not *actually* the best possible. In other words, this objection rested on the view that right and wrong depend, in a sense, upon what the agent *can know.* And in the present chapter I propose to consider objections, which rest, instead of this, upon the view that right and wrong depend upon what the agent *can do.*

Now it must be remembered that, *in a sense,* our original theory does hold and even insists that this is the case. We have, for instance, frequently referred to it in the last chapter as holding that an action is only right, if it produces the best *possible* consequences; and by "the best *possible* consequences" was meant "consequences at least as good as would have followed from any action which the agent *could* have done instead." It does, therefore, hold that the question whether an action is right or wrong does always depend upon a comparison of its consequences with those of all the other actions which the agent *could* have done instead. It assumes, therefore, that wherever a voluntary action is right or wrong (and we have throughout

* From G. E. Moore, *Ethics* (Oxford: The Clarendon Press, 1912), pp. 102–15. Reprinted by permission of the Clarendon Press, Oxford.

only been talking of *voluntary* actions), it is true that the agent *could,* in a sense, have done something else instead. This is an absolutely essential part of the theory.

But the reader must now be reminded that all along we have been using the words "can," "could," and "possible" *in a special sense.* . . . we proposed, purely for the sake of brevity, to say that an agent *could* have done a given action, which he didn't do, wherever it is true that he could have done it, *if* he had chosen; and similarly by what he *can* do, or what is *possible,* we have always meant merely what is possible, *if* he chooses. Our theory, therefore, has not been maintaining, after all, that right and wrong depend upon what the agent absolutely *can* do, but only on what he can do, *if* he chooses. And this makes an immense difference. For, by confining itself in this way, our theory avoids a controversy, which cannot be avoided by those who assert that right and wrong depend upon what the agent absolutely *can* do. There are few, if any, people who will *expressly* deny that we very often really could, *if* we had chosen, have done something different from what we actually did do. But the moment it is asserted that any man ever absolutely *could* have done anything other than what he did do, there are many people who *would* deny this. The view, therefore, which we are to consider in this chapter— the view that right and wrong depend upon what the agent absolutely *can* do—at once involves us in an extremely difficult controversy—the controversy concerning Free Will. There are many people who strenuously deny that any man ever *could* have done anything other than what he actually did do, or ever *can* do anything other than what he *will* do; and there are others who assert the opposite equally strenuously. And whichever view be held is, if *combined* with the view that right and wrong depend upon what the agent absolutely *can* do, liable to contradict our theory very seriously. Those who hold that no man ever *could* have done anything other than what he did do, are, if they *also* hold that right and wrong depend upon what we *can* do, logically bound to hold that no action of ours is ever right and none is ever wrong; and this is a view which is, I think, often actually held, and which, of course, constitutes an extremely serious and fundamental objection to our theory: since our theory implies, on the contrary, that we very often do act *wrongly,* if never quite rightly. Those, on the other hand, who hold that we absolutely *can* do things, which we don't do, and that right and wrong depend upon what we thus *can* do, are also liable to be led to contradict our theory, though for a different reason. Our theory holds that, provided a man could have done something else, *if* he had chosen, that is sufficient to entitle us to say that his action really is either right or wrong. But those who hold the view we are considering will be liable to reply that this is by no means sufficient: that to say that it *is* sufficient, is entirely to misconceive the nature of right and wrong. They will say that, in order that an action may be *really* either right or wrong, it is absolutely essential that the agent should have been *really able* to act differently, able in some sense quite other than that of merely being able, *if* he had chosen. *If* all that were really ever true of us were merely that we could have acted differently, *if* we had chosen, then, these people would say, it really would be true that none of our actions are ever right and that none are ever wrong. They will say, therefore, that our theory entirely misses out one absolutely essential condition of right and wrong—the condition that, for an action to be right or wrong, it must be *freely* done. And moreover, many of them will hold also that the class of actions which we absolutely *can* do is often not identical with those which we can do, *if* we choose. They may say, for instance, that very often an action, which we *could* have done, *if* we had chosen, is nevertheless an action which we *could not* have done; and that an action is always right, if it produces as good consequences as any other action which we really *could* have done instead. From which it will follow that many actions which our theory declares to be *wrong*, will, according to them, be right, because these actions really are the best of all that we *could* have done, though *not* the best of all that we could have done, *if* we had chosen.

Now these objections seem to me to be the most serious which we have yet had to consider. They seem to me to be serious because (1) it is very difficult to be sure that right and wrong do not really depend, as they assert, upon what we *can* do and not merely on what we can do, *if* we choose; and because (2) it is very difficult to be sure in what sense it is true that we ever *could* have done anything different from what we actually did do. I do not profess to be sure about either of these points. And all that I can hope to do is to point out certain facts which do seem to me to be clear, though they are often overlooked; and thus to isolate clearly for the reader's decision, those questions which seem to me to be really doubtful and difficult.

Let us begin with the question: Is it ever true that a man *could* have done anything else, except what he actually did do? And, first of all, I think I had better explain exactly how this question seems to me to be related to the question of Free Will. For it is a fact that, in many discussions about Free Will, this precise question is never mentioned at all; so that it might be thought that the two have really nothing whatever to do with one another. And indeed some philosophers do, I think, definitely imply that they *have* nothing to do with one another: they seem to hold that our wills can properly be said to be free even if we *never* can, in any sense at all, do anything else except what, in the end, we actually do do. But this view, if it is held, seems to me to be plainly a mere abuse of language. The statement that we have Free Will is certainly ordinarily understood to imply that we really sometimes have the power of acting differently from the way in which we actually do act; and hence, if anybody tells us that we have Free Will, while at the same time he means to deny that we ever have such a power, he is simply misleading us. We certainly have *not* got Free Will, in the ordinary sense of the word, if we never really *could,* in any sense at all, have done anything else than what we did do; so that, in this respect, the two questions certainly are connected. But, on the other hand, the mere fact (if it is a fact) that we sometimes *can,* in *some* sense, do what we don't do, does not necessarily entitle us to say that we *have* Free Will. We certainly *haven't* got it, *unless* we can; but it doesn't follow that we *have* got it, even if we *can.* Whether we have or not will depend upon the precise sense in which it is true that we can. So that even if we do decide that we really *can* often, in *some* sense, do what we don't do, this decision by itself does not entitle us to say that we have Free Will.

And the first point about which we can and should be quite clear is, I think, this: namely, that we certainly often *can,* in *some* sense, do what we don't do. It is, I think, quite clear that this is so; and also very important that we should realize that it is so. For many people are inclined to assert, quite without qualification: No man ever *could,* on any occasion, have done anything else than what he actually did do on that occasion. By asserting this quite simply, without qualification, they imply, of course (even if they do not mean to imply), that there is *no* proper sense of the word "could," in which it is true that a man *could* have acted differently. And it is this implication which is, I think, quite certainly absolutely false. For this reason, anybody who asserts, without qualification, "Nothing ever *could* have happened, except what actually did happen," is making an assertion which is quite unjustifiable, and which he himself cannot help constantly contradicting. And it is important to insist on this, because many people do make this unqualified assertion, without seeing how violently it contradicts what they themselves, and all of us, believe, and rightly believe, at other times. If, indeed, they insert a qualification—if they merely say, "In *one* sense of the word '*could*' nothing ever *could* have happened, except what did happen," then, they may perhaps be perfectly right: we are not disputing that they may. All that we are maintaining is that, in *one* perfectly proper and legitimate sense of the world "could," and that one of the very commonest senses in which it is used, it is quite certain that some things which didn't happen *could* have happened. And the proof that this is so, is simply as follows.

It is impossible to exaggerate the frequency of the occasions on which we *all* of us make a distinction between two things, neither of which *did* happen—a distinction which we express by saying, that whereas the one *could* have happened, the other could *not*. No distinction is commoner than this. And no one, I think, who fairly examines the instances in which we make it, can doubt about three things: namely (1) that very often there really is *some* distinction between the two things, corresponding to the language which we use; (2) that this distinction, which really *does* subsist between the things, is *the* one which we mean to express by saying that the one was possible and the other impossible; and (3) that this way of expressing it is a perfectly proper and legitimate way. But if so, it absolutely follows that one of the commonest and most legitimate usages of the phrases "could" and "could not" is to express a difference, which often really does hold between two things *neither* of which did actually happen. Only a few instances need be given. I *could* have walked a mile in twenty minutes this morning, but I certainly could *not* have run two miles in five minutes. I did not, *in fact,* do either of these two things; but it is pure nonsense to say that the mere fact that I *did* not, does away with the distinction between them, which I express by saying that the one *was* within my powers, whereas the other was *not*. *Although* I did neither, yet the one was certainly *possible* to me in a sense in which the other was totally *im*possible. Or, to take another instance: It is true, as a rule, that cats *can* climb trees, whereas dogs *can't*. Suppose that on a particular afternoon neither A's cat nor B's dog *do* climb a tree. It is quite absurd to say that this mere fact proves that we must be wrong if we say (as we certainly often should say) that the cat *could* have climbed a tree, though she didn't, whereas the dog *couldn't*. Or, to take an instance which concerns an inanimate object. Some ships *can* steam twenty knots, whereas others *can't* steam more than fifteen. And the mere fact that, on a particular occasion, a twenty-knot steamer *did* not *actually* run at this speed certainly does not entitle us to say that she *could* not have done so, in the sense in which a fifteen-knot one *could* not. On the contrary, we all can and should distinguish between cases in which (as, for instance, owing to an accident to her propeller) she did not, *because* she could not, and cases in which she did not, *although* she *could*. Instances of this sort might be multiplied quite indefinitely; and it is surely quite plain that we all of us do *continually* use such language: we continually, when considering two events, neither of which *did* happen, distinguish between them by saying that whereas the one *was* possible, though it didn't happen, the other was *im*possible. And it is surely quite plain that what we mean by this (whatever it may be) is something which is often perfectly true. But, if so, then anybody who asserts, without qualification, "Nothing ever *could* have happened, except what did happen," is simply asserting what is false.

It is, therefore, quite certain that we often *could* (in *some* sense) have done what we did not do. And now let us see how this fact is related to the argument by which people try to persuade us that it is *not* a fact.

The argument is well known: it is simply this. It is assumed (for reasons which I need not discuss) that absolutely everything that happens has a *cause* in what precedes it. But to say this is to say that it follows *necessarily* from something that preceded it; or, in other words, that, once the preceding events which are its cause had happened, it was absolutely *bound* to happen. But to say that it was *bound* to happen, is to say that nothing else *could* have happened instead; so that, if *everything* has a cause, *nothing* ever could have happened except what did happen.

And now let us assume that the premise of this argument is correct: that everything really *has* a cause. What really follows from it? Obviously all that follows is that, in *one* sense of the word "could," nothing ever *could* have happened, except what did happen. This really *does* follow. But, if the word "could" is ambiguous—if, that is to say, it is used in different senses on different occasions—it is obviously quite possible that though, in *one* sense, nothing ever could have happened except what did happen, yet in *another* sense, it may at the same time be perfectly true that some things which did not happen *could* have happened. And can anybody undertake to assert with certainty that the word "could" is *not* ambiguous? that it may not have more than one legitimate sense? *Possibly* it is not ambiguous; and, *if* it is not, then the fact that some things, which did not happen, *could* have happened, really would contradict the principle that everything has a cause; and, in that case, we should, I think, have to give up this principle, because the fact that we often *could* have done what we did not do, is so certain. But the assumption that the word "could" is *not* ambiguous is an assumption which certainly should not be made without the clearest proof. And yet I think it often is made, without any proof at all; simply because it does not occur to people that words often are ambiguous. It is, for instance, often assumed, in the Free Will controversy, that the question at issue is solely as to whether everything is caused, or whether acts of will are sometimes uncaused. Those who hold that we *have* Free Will, think themselves bound to maintain that acts of will sometimes have *no* cause; and those who hold that everything is caused think that this proves completely that we have not Free Will. But, in fact, it is extremely doubtful whether Free Will is at all inconsistent with the principle that everything is caused. Whether it is or not, all depends on a very difficult question as to the meaning of the word "could." All that is certain about the matter is (1) that, if we have Free Will, it must be true, in *some* sense, that we sometimes *could* have done, what we did not do; and (2) that, if everything is caused, it must be true, in *some* sense, that we *never could* have done, what we did not do. What is very *un*certain, and what certainly needs to be investigated, is whether these two meanings of the word "could" are the same.

Let us begin by asking: What is the sense of the word "could," in which it is so certain that we often *could* have done, what we did not do? What, for instance, is the sense in which I *could* have walked a mile in twenty minutes this morning, though I did not? There is one suggestion, which is very obvious: namely, that what I mean is simply after all that I could, *if* I had chosen; or (to avoid a possible complication) perhaps we had better say "that I *should, if* I had chosen." In other words, the suggestion is that we often use the phrase *"I could"* simply and solely as a short way of saying "I *should*, if I had chosen." And in all cases, where it is certainly true that we *could* have done, what we did not do, it is, I think, very difficult to be quite sure that this (or something similar) is *not* what we mean by the word "could." The case of the ship may seem to be an exception, because it is certainly not true that she would have steamed twenty knots if *she* had chosen; but even here it seems possible that what we mean is simply that she *would, if the men on board of her* had chosen. There are certainly good reasons for thinking that we *very often* mean by "could" merely "would, *if* so and so had chosen." And if so, then we have a sense of the word "could" in which the fact that we often *could* have done what we did not do, is perfectly compatible with the principle that everything has a cause: for to say that, *if* I had performed a certain act of will, I should have done something which I did not do, in no way contradicts this principle.

And an additional reason for supposing that this *is* what we often mean by "could," and one which is also a reason why it is important to insist on the obvious fact that we very often really *should* have acted differently, *if* we had willed differently, is that those who deny that we ever *could* have done anything, which we did not do, often speak and think as if this really did involve the conclusion that we never should have acted differently, even *if* we had willed differently. This occurs, I think, in two chief instances—one in reference to the future, the other in reference to the past. The first occurs when, because they hold that nothing *can* happen, except what *will* happen, people are led to adopt the view called Fatalism—the view that *whatever we will,* the result will always be the same; that it is, therefore, *never* any use to make one choice rather than another. And this conclusion will really follow if by "can" we mean "*would* happen, even *if* we were to will it." But it is certainly untrue, and it certainly does not follow from the principle of causality. On the contrary, reasons of exactly the same sort and exactly as strong as those which lead us to suppose that everything has a cause, lead to the conclusion that if we choose one course, the result will *always* be different in *some* respect from what it would have been, if we had chosen another; and we know also that the difference would *sometimes* consist in the fact that *what* we chose would come to pass. It is certainly often true of the future, therefore, that whichever of two actions we *were* to choose, *would* actually be done, although it is quite certain that only one of the two *will* be done.

And the second instance, in which people are apt to speak and think, as if, *because* no man ever *could* have done anything but what he did do, it follows that he would not, even *if* he had chosen, is as follows. Many people seem, in fact, to conclude directly from the first of these two propositions, that we can never be justified in praising or blaming a man for anything that he does, or indeed for making any distinction between what is right or wrong, on the one hand, and what is lucky or unfortunate on the other. They conclude, for instance, that there is never any reason to treat or to regard the voluntary commission of a crime in any different way from that in which we treat or regard the involuntary catching of a disease. The man who committed the crime *could* not, they say, have helped committing it any more than the other man could have helped catching the disease; both events were equally inevitable; and though both may of course be great *misfortunes,* though both may have very bad consequences and equally bad ones—there is no justification whatever, they say, for the distinction we make between them when we say that the commission of the crime was *wrong*, or that the man was morally to blame for it, whereas the catching of the disease was *not* wrong and the man was not to blame for it. And this conclusion, again, will really follow if by "*could* not" we mean "*would* not, even if he had willed to avoid it." But the point I want to make is, that it follows *only* if we make this assumption. That is to say, the mere fact that the man *would* have succeeded in avoiding the crime, *if* he had chosen (which is certainly often true), whereas the other man would *not* have succeeded in avoiding the disease, *even* if he had chosen (which is certainly also often true) gives an ample justification for regarding and treating the two cases differently. It gives such a justification, because, where the occurrence of an event *did* depend upon the will, there, by acting on the will (as we may do by blame or punishment) we have often a reasonable chance of preventing similar events from recurring in the future; whereas, where it did *not* depend upon the will, we have no such chance. We may, therefore, fairly say that those who speak and think, as if a man who brings about a misfortune *voluntarily* ought to be treated and regarded in exactly the same way as one who brings about an equally great misfortune *involuntarily,* are speaking and thinking *as if* it were not true that we ever should have acted differently, even *if* we had willed to do so. And that is why it is extremely important to insist on the absolute certainty of the fact that we often really *should* have acted differently, *if* we had willed differently.

There is, therefore, much reason to think that when we say that we *could* have done a thing which we did not do, we *often* mean merely that we *should* have done it, *if* we had chosen. And if so, then it is quite certain that, in *this* sense, we often really *could* have done what we did not do, and that this fact is in no way inconsistent with the principle that everything has a cause. And for my part I must confess that I cannot feel certain that this may not be *all* that we usually mean and understand by the assertion that we have Free Will; so that those who deny that we have it are really denying (though, no doubt, often unconsciously) that we ever *should* have acted differently, even if we had willed differently. It has been sometimes held that this *is* what we mean; and I cannot find any conclusive argument to the contrary. And if it is what we mean, then it absolutely follows that we really *have* Free Will, and also that this fact is quite consistent with the principle that everything has a cause; and it follows also that our theory will be perfectly right, when it makes right and wrong depend on what we *could* have done, *if* we had chosen.

But, no doubt, there are many people who will say that this is *not* sufficient to entitle us to say that we have Free Will; and they will say this for a reason, which certainly has some plausibility, though I cannot satisfy myself that it is conclusive. They will say, namely: Granted that we often *should* have acted differently, *if* we had chosen differently, yet it is not true that we have Free Will, unless it is *also* often true in such cases that we *could* have *chosen* differently. The question of Free Will has been thus represented as being merely the question whether we ever *could* have chosen, what we did not choose, or ever *can* choose, what, in fact, we shall not choose. And since there is some plausibility in this contention, it is, I think, worthwhile to point out that here again it is absolutely certain that, in two different senses, at least, we often *could* have chosen, what, in fact, we did not choose; and that in neither sense does this fact contradict the principle of causality.

The first is simply the old sense over again. If by saying that we *could* have done, what we did not do, we often mean merely that we *should* have done it, *if* we had chosen to do it, then obviously, by saying that we *could* have *chosen* to do it, we may mean merely that we *should* have so chosen, *if* we had chosen *to make the choice*. And I think there is no doubt it is often true that we should have chosen to do a particular thing *if* we had chosen to make the choice; and that this is a very important sense in which it is often in our power to make a choice. There certainly is such a thing as making an effort to induce ourselves to *choose* a particular course; and I think there is no doubt that often if we *had* made such an effort, we *should* have made a choice, which we did not in fact make.

And besides this, there is another sense in which, whenever we have several different courses of action in view, it is *possible* for us to choose any one of them; and a sense which is certainly of some practical importance, even if it goes no way to justify us in saying that we have Free Will. This sense arises from the fact that in such cases we can hardly ever *know for certain* beforehand, *which* choice we actually *shall* make; and one of the commonest senses of the word "possible" is that in which we call an event "possible" when no man can *know for certain* that it will *not* happen. It follows that almost, if not quite always, when we make a choice, after considering alternatives, it *was* possible that we should have chosen one of these alternatives, which we did not actually choose; and often, of course, it was not only possible, but highly probable, that we should have done so. And this fact is certainly of practical importance, because many people are apt much too easily to assume that it is quite certain that they *will not* make a given choice, which they know they ought to make, if it were possible; and their belief that they *will* not make it tends, of course, to prevent them from making it. For this reason it is important to insist that they can hardly ever know for certain with regard to any given choice that they will *not* make it.

It is, therefore, quite certain (1) that we often *should* have *acted* differently, if we had chosen to; (2) that similarly we often should have *chosen* differently, *if* we had chosen so to choose; and (3) that it was almost always *possible* that we should have chosen differently, in the sense that no man could know for certain that we should *not* so choose. All these three things are facts, and all of them are quite consistent with the principle of causality. Can anybody undertake to say for certain that none of these three facts and *no* combination of them will justify us in saying that we have Free Will? Or, suppose it granted that we have not Free Will, unless it is often true that we *could* have chosen, what we did not choose: Can any defender of Free Will, or any opponent of it, show conclusively that what he means by "*could* have chosen" in this proposition, is anything different from the two certain facts, which I have numbered (2) and (3), or some combination of the two? Many people, no doubt, will still insist that these two facts alone are by no means sufficient to entitle us to say that we have Free Will: that it must be true that we were *able* to choose, in some quite other sense. But nobody, so far as I know, has ever been able to tell us exactly what that sense is. For my part, I can find no conclusive argument to show either that some such other sense of "can" is necessary, or that it is not. And, therefore, this chapter must conclude with a doubt. It is, I think, possible that, instead of saying, as our theory said, that an action is only right, when it produces consequences as good as any which would have followed from any other action which the agent *would* have done, *if* he had chosen, we should say instead that it is right whenever and only when the agent *could not have done* anything which would have produced better consequences: and that this "*could not have done*" is *not* equivalent to "would not have done, *if* he had chosen," but is to be understood in the sense, whatever it may be, which is sufficient to entitle us to say that we have Free Will. If so, then our theory would be wrong, just to this extent.

STEPHEN N. THOMAS

A Modal Muddle

~~~~~~

In his book *Ethics,* G. E. Moore cited an argument by which, he says, people try to persuade us that it is never true that we could have done otherwise than we did.[1] He said:

> The argument is well known: it is simply this. It is assumed (for reasons which I need not discuss) that absolutely everything that happens has a *cause* in what precedes it. But to say this is to say that it follows necessarily from something that preceded it; or in other words, that once the preceding events which are its cause had happened, it was absolutely *bound* to happen. But to say that it was *bound* to happen, is to say that nothing else could have happened instead; so that, if *everything* has a cause, nothing ever could have happened except what did happen.[2]

Moore was apparently convinced by this argument; if, he says, we grant the premise that "everything has a cause," it "really follows" that nothing ever could have happened except what did happen.[3]

But Moore naturally did not wish to accept any conclusion with negative implications for ascriptions of moral responsibility. He tried to ward off this threat by suggesting that the word "could" may possibly have several senses and that there may be a special sense of the word "could" for which it will *not* be the case that the claim that

---

* A previously unpublished paper.
[1] G. E. Moore, *Ethics* (New York: Oxford University Press, 1965), p. 89.
[2] *Ibid.,* p. 89.
[3] *Ibid.,* p. 89.

"everything has a cause" implies "we could never act otherwise than we do." In particular, Moore suggested that there may be a sense of the word "could" in which to say, "I could have done otherwise" means "I should, if I had chosen." [4]

This suggestion has been attacked from many quarters. Some philosophers have said that it was absurd to say that the phrase "could have" ever means "should have if I had chosen." [5] Other philosophers have criticized Moore on the grounds that even if the claim that someone "could have done otherwise" were understood to mean "could have done otherwise *if* he had so chosen," this still would not constitute sufficient grounds for the ascription of moral responsibility since, for example, the man who is forced at gunpoint to do something "could have done otherwise if he had so chosen," and yet we would not hold him morally responsible for what he did.[6] (Of course, it is doubtful that Moore ever considered this a *sufficient* condition for the ascription of moral responsibility.)

None of these critics, however, questioned the validity of the original argument which lead Moore to make this suggestion. The present paper discusses the validity of that argument and others like it which purport to show that "Everything has a cause" implies "We could never act otherwise than we do."

Use of the notion of a "modal operator" will facilitate the present discussion. The notion is very simple. We introduce the symbol "$\square$" which is thought of as governing a sentence—for example

$$\square \, (p)$$

and which has the effect of signalling that the sentence it governs is (or is alleged to be) the expression of a "necessary truth." For example,

$$\square \, (7 + 5 = 12).$$

The sentence governed by a modal operator is said to lie in the "scope" of that operator. For example, in the case of

[4] *Ibid.*, p. 90.

[5] J. L. Austin, "Ifs and Cans," in J. O. Urmson and G. J. Warnock, eds., *Philosophical Papers* (London: Oxford University Press, 1961), p. 156.

[6] C. A. Campbell, "Is Free Will a Pseudo-Problem?" *Mind*, LX (1951), p. 444.

$$\Box \ (\text{p or q})$$

the whole disjunction, "p or q" lies in the scope of the necessity operator. This, of course, is not the same thing as a disjunction of these two sentences each governed by a necessity operator

$$\Box \ (\text{p}) \quad \text{or} \quad \Box \ (\text{q}).$$

The matter of correctly fixing the scope of a modal operator will be important later on.

We may also introduce a "possibility operator," "O", which, when applied to a sentence "p"

$$O(\text{p})$$

marks "p" as "possibly true"—for example, that "p" is not self-contradictory and so *may* be true. The necessity operator and the possibility operator are obviously related since if a sentence is necessarily false

$$\Box \ (\text{not-p})$$

then it is not possible that it is true

$$\text{not } O(\text{p})$$

and *vice versa*.

Let us now consider the following argument:

> (1) Given that the factors which caused a man to act as he did existed, he could not have acted otherwise.
> (2) Those factors existed.

> ∴ (3) He could not have acted otherwise.
> ∴ He did not act of his own free will.
> (and)   ∴ He cannot legitimately be held morally responsible.

The same argument can be cast in different forms, but this example will serve for present purposes.

Let us compare and contrast the above argument with the following argument:

> (1) If a vase is in perfect condition, then it cannot be broken or cracked.
> (2) My vase is in perfect condition.

> ∴ (3) My vase cannot be broken or cracked.
> ∴ My vase is unbreakable.

Plainly there is something wrong with this argument.

Among other things, something strange seems to have gone on with the term "could" or "can" in the course of the argument. I think it is this:

In the first premise, in the sense in which we take it when we agree to it, the term "could" or "can" functions as a modal operator governing the whole conditional

$$\square \text{ (if p then q).}$$

That is, it means something like

> Necessarily: If a vase is in perfect condition, then it is not broken or cracked.
> Necessarily: If the factors which caused a man to act as he did existed, he did not act otherwise.

where if we assent to these "necessary truths," we probably do so because we would assent to:

> It follows logically that: If a vase. . . .
> It follows logically that: If the factors . . .

—that is, because the antecedent of the conditional, as we understand it, entails the consequent.

But then, in the course of the argument, it becomes clear that these statements are not being treated as if they were of the form

$$\square \text{ (if p then q)}$$

but rather as if they were of the form

$$\text{if p then } \square(q)$$

since the inference seems to be of the form

$$\text{if p then } \square(q)$$
$$\frac{p}{\square(q)}$$

whereas the inference

$$\square \text{ (if p then q)}$$
$$\frac{p}{\square(q)}.$$

would not be a valid inference (although we would, of course, be entitled to infer just "q"—that is, "My vase is not broken or cracked" and "He did not act otherwise").

How does it come about that the scope of the modal operator gets misinterpreted with the result that necessity appears to be associated with the conclusion? It comes about, perhaps, in the following way. The word "could" in English—as well as a number of other words, like "must", for example—in at least some of its uses performs essentially the same function as a modal operator. The word "could," for example, may function as a possibility operator

(A) It could be the case that p.

And when combined with the particle "not"

(B) It could not be the case that p.

it functions, as such sentences are usually understood, to say

Not possible that p

or: not O(p)

that is, it is equivalent to a necessity operator

Necessarily not-p

that is: $\Box$ (not p).

[Sentence (B) might also be read

It could (not be the case that p)
i.e. Possible that not-p

but this would be a very unusual reading.]

But the feature of English (as well as many other natural languages) which may lead us into confusion is that in English, *the word "could" when it expresses a modal operator which governs a whole conditional may nevertheless be put into one of the clauses of the conditional.* This happens, for example, in the sentence

If a vase is in perfect condition, then it cannot be broken or cracked.

Here "cannot," although it expresses a necessity operator governing the whole conditional, nonetheless is placed in the clause expressing the consequent. The same thing happens in

> Given that the factors which caused a man to act as he did existed, he could not have acted otherwise.

And it may be that failing to notice this, an argument was constructed in which the phrase "could not" was treated as if it expressed a modal operator governing *only* the consequent of the conditional

$$\text{if p then } \Box q$$
$$\frac{p}{\Box q}$$

This particular error in reasoning seems never to be mentioned in logic books. Let us therefore call it "the fallacy of misconstruing the scope of the modal operator."

But now it may be asked: Why count this as "a fallacy of misconstruing the scope of the modal operator"? That is, why should we think of the error as arising from *an incorrect reading* of the English as

$$\text{if p then } \Box q$$

and *not* think of it as involving a correct construal of the scope of the modal operator but an invalid argument form:

(invalid)
$$\frac{\Box \text{ (if p then q)}}{\quad p \quad}$$
$$\Box q$$

Perhaps no iron-clad reasons can be given for analyzing the error one way rather than the other. But by considering the error here to come from "misconstruing the scope of the modal operator," we can group these arguments under the same heading with other arguments which, intuitively, seem to commit the "same" fallacy. For example, there is the skeptical argument against the possibility of knowledge: [7]

---

[7] Norman Malcolm concerns himself with a very similar argument in his book *Knowledge and Certainty*. Like Moore, he never questions the validity of the argument but tries to avoid its conclusion by suggesting that there may be

If you know something, then you cannot be wrong about it.
But you can be wrong about anything.

There is nothing that you know.

The argument form here is different from the form of the earlier arguments. The second premise serves to deny the necessity of the consequent of the first premise:

if p then $\Box$ (not-q)
O(q)
∴ not: $\Box$ (not-q)   (intermediate conclusion)

∴ not-p.

If we say that the error came in *construing* the first premise to be of the form

if p then $\Box$ (not-q)

when it was actually

$\Box$ (if you know something, then
you are not wrong about it)

then we can say that this argument, although different in logical form, commits the *same* fallacy.

A second query which may be raised is this: Is it not strange to suggest that the proponents of the original argument *thought* that "A man can never do otherwise than he did" is logically necessary? This would be a strange thing to suggest; but the present suggestion is that the "necessity" which they associate with the conclusion and which they interpret, in their informal reasoning, as some special form of "necessity" associated peculiarly with *causation* is really only, so to speak, logical necessity misplaced. But it still remains open to someone to try to explicate a notion of "necessity," say "physical necessity," such that in the argument

(1) If Jones' doing X was caused, then it was not *physically possible* that Jones not have done X.

---

a "special sense" of, in this case, the word "know" for which it will not be the case that " 'It could have turned out that I was mistaken' implies 'I did not know.' " Cf. *Knowledge and Certainty* (Englewood Cliffs, N.J.: Prentice-Hall, Inc., 1963), pp. 60–61.

(2) If Jones is morally responsible for doing X, then it must have been *physically possible* for him not to have done X.

(3) Jones' doing X was caused.

∴. Jones is not morally responsible for doing X.

premises (1) and (2) are true and the argument follows. Some "explication" is certainly required since without it we have no reason to think the argument is any different from the plainly fallacious

(1) If the automobile's not starting was caused, then it was not physically possible that it have been started.

(2) If the automobile was in working condition, it must have been physically possible for it to have been started.

(3) Smith's failure to pull the choke caused the automobile's not starting.

∴. The automobile was not in working condition.

I do not say that no concept of "physical necessity" satisfying all these conditions exists. But I suspect that people are led to think that there must be such a concept by a misinterpretation of the "must" in "If something is caused to occur, then it *must* occur."

C. D. BROAD

Determinism,
Indeterminism,
and Libertarianism

~~~~~~

THE IMPLICATIONS OF OBLIGABILITY

We often make retrospective judgments about the past actions of
ourselves or other people which take the form: "You ought not to
have done the action X, which you in fact did; you ought instead to
have done the action Y, which in fact you did not." If I make such
a judgment about a person, and he wants to refute it, he can take
two different lines of argument. (1) He may say: "I could have done
Y instead of X, but you are mistaken in thinking that Y was the action that I ought to have done. In point of fact, X, the action that
I did, was the one that I ought to have done. If I had done Y, I
should have done what I ought not to have done." (2) He may say:
"I could not help doing X," or he may say: "Though I need not
have done X, I could not possibly have done Y."

If the accused person makes an answer of the first kind, he is admitting that the alternatives "ought" and "ought not" apply to the
actions X and Y, but he is objecting to my applying "ought" to Y
and "ought not" to X. He is saying that "ought" applies to X, and
"ought not" to Y. It is as if two people, who agree that X and Y are
each either black or white, should differ because one holds that X
is black and Y white whilst the other holds that X is white and Y
black. If the accused person makes an answer of the second kind, he

---

* From C. D. Broad, *Ethics and the History of Philosophy* (London: Routledge
& Kegan Paul Ltd., 1952), pp. 195–217. Reprinted by permission of the publishers.

is denying the applicability of the alternatives "ought" and "ought not." If he says: "I could not help doing X," he assumes that his critic will admit that neither "ought" nor "ought not" has any application to an action which the agent could not help doing. If he says: "Though I need not have done X, yet I could not possibly have done Y," he assumes that his critic will admit that neither "ought" nor "ought not" has any application to an action which the agent could not have done. It is as if one person should say that X is black and Y is white, and the other should answer that at least one of them is unextended and therefore incapable of being either black or white.

OBLIGABILITY ENTAILS SUBSTITUTABILITY

Now we are concerned here only with the second kind of answer. The essential point to notice is that it is universally admitted to be a *relevant* answer. We all admit that there is some sense or other of "could" in which "ought" and "ought not" entail "could." We will now try to get clear about the connexion between these two notions.

Judgments of obligation about past actions may be divided into two classes, namely (1) judgments about actions which were actually done, and (2) judgments about conceivable actions which were not done. Each divides into two sub-classes, and so we get the following fourfold division. (1·1) "You did X, and X was the action that you ought to have done." (1·2) "You did X, and X was an action that you ought not to have done." (2·1) "You did not do X, and X was the action that you ought to have done." And (2·2) "You did not do X, and X was an action that you ought not to have done." Now both judgments of the first class entail that you could have helped doing the action which you in fact did. If the action that you did can be said to be one that you ought to have done, or if it can be said to be one that you ought not to have done, it must be one that you *need not* have done. And, since you actually did it, it is obviously one that you *could have* done. Both judgments of the second class entail that you could have done an action which you did not in fact do. If a conceivable action which you did not do can be said to be one which you ought to have done, or if it can be said to be one that you ought not to have done, it must be one that you *could have* done. And, since you actually failed to do it, it is obviously one that you *need not* have done.

It is worth while to notice that the common phrases: "You ought to have done so and so" and "You ought not to have done so and so" are generally equivalent to our judgments $(2 \cdot 1)$ and $(1 \cdot 2)$ respectively. The former is generally used to mean: "You did not do so and so, and that was an action which you ought to have done." The latter is generally used to mean: "You did so and so, and that was an action which you ought not to have done." But we often need to express what is expressed by our judgments $(1 \cdot 1)$ and $(2 \cdot 2)$. We often want to say that a person did what he ought on a certain occasion, and we often want to say that a person avoided doing something which he ought not to have done on a certain occasion. For this is exactly the state of affairs which exists when a person has in fact done an unpleasant duty in face of a strong temptation to shirk it by lying.

Now the importance of this connexion between "ought" and "ought not," on the one hand, and "could," on the other, is very great. People constantly make judgments of obligation of the four kinds which we have distinguished, and such judgments have constantly been made throughout the whole course of human history. Every single one of these judgments has been false unless there have been cases in which actions which *were* done could have been left undone and actions which *were not* done could have been done. And these judgments would all have been false in principle, and not merely in detail. They would have been false, not in the sense that thy asserted "ought" where they should have asserted "ought not," or *vice versa*. They would be false in the sense that nothing in the world has ever had that determinable characteristic of which "ought to be done" and "ought not to be done" are the determinate specifications. They would be false in the sense in which all judgments which predicated redness, blueness, and so forth, of any object would be false in a world which contained no objects except minds and noises.

It will be convenient to call an action "obligable" if and only if it is an action of which "ought to be done" or "ought not to be done" can be predicated. It will be convenient to call an action "substitutable" if either it was done but could have been left undone, or it was left undone but could have been done. We may then sum up the situation by saying that an action is obligable if and only if it is, in a certain sense, substitutable; that, unless all judgments of obligation are false in principle, there are obligable actions; and therefore, unless all judgments of obligation are false in principle, there are actions which are, in this sense, substitutable.

VARIOUS SENSES OF "SUBSTITUTABLE"

This is one aspect of the case. The other aspect is the following. There are several senses of "could" in which nearly everyone would admit that some actions which were done could have been left undone, and some actions which were left undone could have been done. There are thus several senses of "substitutable" in which it would commonly be admitted that some actions are substitutable. But, although an action which was *not* substitutable in these senses would *not* be obligable, it seems doubtful whether an action which was substitutable *only* in these senses *would be* obligable. It seems doubtful whether an action would be obligable unless it were substitutable in some further sense.

At this stage two difficulties arise. (i) It is extremely difficult to grasp and to express clearly this further sense of "substitutable," that is, this further sense of "could" in which an action that was done could have been left undone or an action which was not done could have been done. Many people would say that they can attach no meaning to "substitutable" except those meanings in which it is insufficient to make an action obligable. (ii) Even if this other meaning of "substitutable" can be grasped and clearly expressed, many people would say that no action is substitutable in this sense. They would claim to see that no action which has been done could have been left undone, and that no action which was not done could have been done, in that sense of "could" which is required if an action is to be obligable.

Now anyone who holds these views is in a very awkward position. On the one hand, it is not easy to believe that every judgment of obligation is false, in the sense in which every judgment ascribing colour to an object would be false in a world containing only minds and noises. On the other hand, it is highly depressing to have to admit that there is a sense of "could" which you can neither grasp nor clearly express. And it is equally unsatisfactory to have to believe that some actions *are* substitutable in a sense in which it seems to you self-evident that no action *could be* substitutable.

There are two problems to be tackled at this point. (i) To try to discover and state the sense of "substitutable" in which being substitutable is the necessary and sufficient condition of being obligable. And (ii), if we can do this, to consider whether any action could be substitutable in this sense.

VOLUNTARY SUBSTITUTABILITY

Let us begin by considering an action which has actually been performed. In some cases we should say that the agent "could not have helped" performing it. We should certainly say this if we had reason to believe that the very same act would have been performed by the agent in these circumstances even though he had willed that it should not take place. It is obvious that there are actions which are "inevitable," in this sense, since there are actions which take place although the agent is trying his hardest to prevent them. Compare, for example, the case of a conspirator taken with an uncontrollable fit of sneezing.

Next consider a conceivable action which was not in fact performed. In some cases we should say that the agent "could not possibly" have performed it. We should certainly say this if the act would not have taken place in these circumstances no matter how strongly the agent had willed it. It is obvious that there are conceivable acts which are "impossible" in this sense, since there are cases where such an act fails to take place although the agent is trying his hardest to bring it about. Compare, for example, the case of a man who is bound and gagged, and tries vainly to give warning to a friend.

We will call acts of these two kinds "not voluntarily substitutable." It is plain that an act which is not voluntarily substitutable is not obligable. No one would say that the conspirator ought not to have sneezed, or that the bound and gagged man ought to have warned his friend. At most we may be able to say that they ought or ought not to have done certain things in the past which are relevant to their present situation. Perhaps the conspirator ought to have sprayed his nose with cocaine before hiding behind the presumably dusty arras, and perhaps the victim ought not to have let himself be lured into the house in which he was gagged and bound. But these are previous questions.

We see then that to be voluntarily substitutable is a *necessary* condition for an action to be obligable. But is it a *sufficient* condition? Suppose I performed the action A on a certain occasion. Suppose that I should not have done A then if I had willed with a certain degree of force and persistence not to do it. Since I did A, it is certain that I *did not* will with this degree of force and persistence to avoid doing it. Now suppose that at the time I *could not* have willed with this degree of force and persistence to avoid doing A. Should we be prepared to say that I ought not to have done A?

Now take another case. Suppose that on a certain occasion I failed to do a certain conceivable action B. Suppose that I should have done B if I had willed with a certain degree of force and persistence to do it. Since I did not do B, it is certain that I *did not* will with this degree of force and persistence to do it. Now suppose that at the time I *could not* have willed with this degree of force and persistence to do B. Should we be prepared to say that I ought to have done B? It seems to me almost certain that, under the supposed conditions, we should not be prepared to say either that I ought not to have done A or that I ought to have done B.

Consider, for example, the case of a man who gradually becomes addicted to some drug like morphine, and eventually becomes a slave to it. At the early stages we should probably hold that he could have willed with enough force and persistence to ensure that the temptation would be resisted. At the latest stages we should probably hold that he could not have done so. Now at every stage, from the earliest to the latest, the hypothetical proposition would be true: "If he had willed with a certain degree of force and persistence to avoid taking morphine, he would have avoided taking it." Yet we should say at the earlier stages that he ought to have resisted, whilst, at the final stages, we should be inclined to say that "ought" and "ought not" have ceased to apply.

PRIMARY AND SECONDARY SUBSTITUTABILITY

An action which was in fact done, but would not have been done if there had been a strong and persistent enough desire in the agent not to do it, will be called "primarily avoidable." Suppose, in addition, that there could have been in the agent at the time a desire of sufficient strength and persistence to prevent the action being done. Then the action might be called "secondarily avoidable." If this latter condition is not fulfilled, we shall say that the action was "primarily avoidable, but secondarily inevitable." Similarly, an action which was not in fact done, but would have been done if there had been in the agent a strong and persistent enough desire to do it, will be called "primarily possible." Suppose in addition, that there could have been in the agent at the time a desire of sufficient strength and persistence to ensure the action being done. Then the action may be called "secondarily possible." If this latter condition is not fulfilled, we shall say that the action is "primarily possible, but secondarily impossible." An action will be called "primarily substitutable" if it is either primarily avoidable or primarily possible. It will be "secondarily substitutable" if it is either secondarily avoidable or secondarily possible. In order that an action may be obligable it is not enough that it should be primarily substitutable, it must be at least secondarily substitutable.

We are thus led on from the notion of voluntarily substitutable *actions* to that of substitutable *volitions*. Suppose that, on a certain occasion and in a certain situation, a certain agent willed a certain alternative with a certain degree of force and persistence. We may say that the volition was substitutable if the same agent, on the same occasion and in the same circumstances, could instead have willed a different alternative or could have willed the same alternative with a different degree of force and persistence. Now there is one sense of "could" in which it might plausibly be suggested that many volitions are substitutable. It seems very likely that there are many occasions on which I *should* have willed otherwise than I did *if* on previous occasions I had willed otherwise than I did. So it seems likely that many volitions have been voluntarily substitutable.

It is necessary to be careful at this point, or we may be inadvertently granting more than we are really prepared to admit. Obviously it is often true that, if I had willed otherwise than I did on certain earlier occasions, I should never have got into the position in which I afterwards made a certain decision. If, for example, Julius Caesar had decided earlier in his career not to accept the command in Gaul, he would never have been in the situation in which he decided to cross the Rubicon. This, however, does not make his decision to cross the Rubicon substitutable. For a volition is substitutable only if a different volition could have occurred in the agent in the *same* situation. Again, it is often true that, if I had willed otherwise than I did on certain earlier occasions, my state of knowledge and belief would have been different on certain later occasions from what it in fact was. In that case I should have thought, on these later occasions, of certain alternatives which I did not and could not think of in my actual state of knowledge and belief. Suppose, for example, that a lawyer has to decide what to do when a friend has met with an accident. If this man had decided years before to study medicine instead of law, it is quite likely that he would now think of, and perhaps choose, an alternative which his lack of medical knowledge prevents him from contemplating. This, however, does not make the lawyer's volition in the actual situation substitutable. For, although the external part of the total situation might have been the same whether he had previously decided to study medicine or to study law, the internal part of the total situation would have been different if he had decided to study medicine, instead of deciding, as he did, to study law. He would have become an agent with different cognitive powers and dispositions from those which he in fact has. No one would think of saying that the lawyer ought to have done a certain action, which he did not and could not contemplate, merely because he would have contemplated it and would have decided to do it if he had decided years before to become a doctor instead of becoming a lawyer.

Having cleared these irrelevances away, we can now come to the real point. A man's present conative-emotional dispositions, and what we may call his "power of intense and persistent willing," are in part dependent on his earlier volitions. If a person has repeatedly chosen the easier of the alternatives open to him, it becomes increasingly difficult for him to choose and to persist in pursuing the harder of two alternatives. If he has formed a habit of turning his attention away from certain kinds of fact, it will become increasingly difficult for him to attend fairly to alternatives which involve facts of these kinds. This is one aspect of the case. Another, and equally important, aspect is the following. If a man reflects on his own past decisions, he may see that he has a tendency to ignore or to dwell upon certain kinds of fact, and that this had led him to make unfair or unwise decisions on many occasions. He may decide that, in future, he will make a special effort to give due, and not more than due, weight to those considerations which he has a tendency to ignore or to dwell upon. And this decision may make a difference to his future decisions. On the other hand, he may see that certain alternatives have a specially strong attraction for him, and he may find that, if he pays more than a fleeting attention to them, he will be rushed into choosing them, and will afterwards regret it. He may decide that, in future, he will think as little as possible about such alternatives. And this decision may make a profound difference to his future decisions.

We can now state the position in general terms. Suppose that, if the agent had willed differently on earlier occasions, his conative-emotional dispositions and his knowledge of his own nature would have been so modified that he would now have willed differently in the actual external situation and in his actual state of knowledge and belief about the alternatives open to him. Then we can say that his actual volition in the present situation was "voluntarily avoidable," and that a volition of a different kind or of a different degree of force and persistence was "voluntarily possible." An action which took place was secondarily avoidable if the following two conditions are fulfilled. (i) That this action would not have been done if the agent had willed with a certain degree of force and persistence to avoid it. (ii) That, if he had willed differently in the past, his conative-emotional dispositions and his knowledge of his own nature would have been such, at the time when he did the action, that he would have willed to avoid it with enough force and persistence to prevent him doing it. In a precisely similar way we could define the statement that a certain conceivable action, which was not done, was secondarily possible. And we can thus define the statement that an action is secondarily substitutable.

Can we say that an action is obligable if it is secondarily substitutable, in the sense just defined, though it is not obligable if it is only primarily substitutable? It seems to me that the same difficulty which we noticed before reappears here. Suppose that the agent could not have willed otherwise than he did in the remoter past. It is surely irrelevant to say that, *if* he had done so, his conative dispositions *would* have been different at a later stage from what they in fact were then, and that he *would* have willed otherwise than he then did. One might, of course, try to deal with this situation by referring back to still earlier volitions. One might talk of actions which are not only primarily, or only secondarily, but are tertiarily substitutable. But it is quite clear that this is useless. If neither primary nor secondary substitutability, in the sense defined, suffice to make an action obligable, no higher order of substitutability, in this sense, will suffice. The further moves are of exactly the same nature as the second move. And so, if the second move does not get us out of the difficulty, none of the further moves will do so.

CATEGORICAL SUBSTITUTABILITY

The kind of substitutability which we have so far considered may be called "conditional substitutability." For at every stage we have defined "could" to mean "would have been, if certain conditions had been fulfilled which were not." Now I have concluded that merely conditional substitutability, of however high an order, is not a sufficient condition for obligability. If an action is to be obligable, it must be *categorically* substitutable. We must be able to say of an action, which was done, that it could have been avoided, in some sense of "could" which is not definable in terms of "would have, if." And we must be able to say of a conceivable action, which was not done, that it could have been done, in some sense of "could" which is not definable in terms of "would have, if." Unless there are some actions of which such things can truly be said, there are no actions which are obligable. We must therefore consider whether any clear meaning can be attached to the phrase "categorically substitutable," that is, whether "could" has any clear meaning except "would have, if." And, if we can find such a meaning, we must enquire whether any actions are categorically substitutable.

VARIOUS SENSES OF "OBLIGABLE"

Before tackling these questions I must point out that the words "ought" and "ought not" are used in several different senses. In some of these senses obligability does not entail categorical substitutability.

(i) There is a sense of "ought" in which we apply it even to inanimate objects. It would be quite proper to say: "A car ought to be able to get from London to Cambridge in less than three hours," or: "A fountain-pen ought not to be constantly making blots." We mean by this simply that a car which did take more than three hours would be a poor specimen of car, or would be in a bad state of repair. And similar remarks apply to the statement about the fountain-pen. We are comparing the behaviour of a certain car or fountain-pen with the average standard of achievement of cars or fountain-pens. We are not suggesting that *this* car or *this* pen, in its present state of repair, unconditionally could go faster or avoid making blots. Sometimes when we make such judgments we are comparing an individual's achievements, not with those of the *average* member, but with those of an *ideally perfect* member, of a certain class to which it belongs. We will call "ought," in this sense, "the comparative ought." And we can then distinguish "the average-comparative ought" and "the ideal-comparative ought."

(ii) Plainly "ought" and "ought not" can be, and often are, used in this sense of human actions. But, in the case of human actions, there is a further development. Since a human being has the power of cognition, in general, and of reflexive cognition, in particular, he can have an idea of an average or an ideal man. He can compare his own achievements with those of the average, or the ideal, man, as conceived by him. And he will have a more or less strong and persistent desire to approximate to the ideal and not to fall below the average. Now it is part of the notion of an ideal man that he is a being who would have a high ideal of human nature and would desire strongly and persistently to approximate to his ideal. Obviously it is no part of the notion of an ideal horse or an ideal car that it is a being which would have a high ideal of horses or cars and a strong and persistent desire to live up to this. When we say that a man ought not to cheat at cards we often mean to assert two things. (a) That the average decent man does not do this, and that anyone who does falls in this respect below the average. And (b) that a man who does this either has a very low ideal of human nature or a very weak and unstable desire to approximate to the ideal which he has. So that, in this further respect, he falls below the average.

Now neither of these judgments implies that a particular person, who cheated on a particular occasion, categorically could have avoided cheating then; or that he categorically could have had a higher ideal of human nature; or that he categorically could have willed more strongly and persistently to live up to the ideal which he had. For an action to be obligable, in this sense, it is plain enough that it should be secondarily substitutable, in the sense already defined.

THE CATEGORICAL OUGHT

Some philosophers of great eminence, for example Spinoza, have held that the sense of "ought" which I have just discussed is the only sense of it. Plainly it is a very important sense, and it is one in which "ought" and "ought not" can be applied only to the actions of intelligent beings with power of reflexive cognition, emotion, and conation. I think that a clear-headed Determinist should hold either that this is the only sense; or that, if there is another sense, in which obligability entails *categorical* substitutability, it has no application.

Most people, however, would say that, although we often do use "ought" and "ought not" in this sense, we quite often use them in another sense, and that in this other sense they entail categorical substitutability. I am inclined to think that this is true. When I judge that I ought not to have done something which I in fact did, I do not as a rule seem to be judging merely that a person with higher ideals, or with a stronger and more persistent desire to live up to his ideals, would not have done what I did. Even when this is part of what I mean, there seems to be something more implied in my judgment, namely that I *could* have had higher ideals or *could* have willed more strongly and persistently to live up to my ideals, where "could" does not mean just "would have, if." Let us call this sense of "ought" the "categorical ought." It seems to me then that we must distinguish between an action being obligable in the comparative sense and being obligable in the categorical sense; and that, if any action were categorically obligable, it would have to be categorically substitutable.

ANALYSIS OF CATEGORICAL SUBSTITUTABILITY

We can now proceed to discuss the notion of categorical substitutability. It seems to me to involve a negative and a positive condition. I think that the negative condition can be clearly formulated, and that there is no insuperable difficulty in admitting that it may sometimes be fulfilled. The ultimate difficulty is to give any intelligible account of the positive condition. I will now explain and illustrate these statements.

Suppose that, on a certain occasion, I willed a certain alternative with a certain degree of force and persistence, and that, in consequence of this volition, I did a certain voluntary action which I should not have done unless I had willed this alternative with this degree of intensity and persistence. To say that I categorically could have avoided doing this action implies at least that the following negative condition is fulfilled. It implies that the process of my willing this alternative with this degree of force and persistence was not completely determined by the nomic, the occurrent, the dispositional, and the background conditions which existed immediately before and during this process of willing. In order to see exactly what this means it will be best to contrast it with a case in which we believe that a process is completely determined by such conditions.

Suppose that two billiard-balls are moving on a table, that they collide at a certain moment, and that they go on moving in modified directions with modified velocities in consequence of the impact. Let us take as universal premises the general laws of motion and of elastic impact. We will call these "nomic premises." Let us take as singular premises the following propositions. (i) That each ball was moving in such and such a direction and with such and such a velocity at the moment of impact. We will call this an "occurrent premiss." (ii) That the masses and coefficients of elasticity of the balls were such and such. We will call this a "dispositional premiss." (iii) That the table was smooth and level before, at, and after the moment of impact. We will call this a "background premiss." Lastly, let us take the proposition that the balls are moving, directly after the impact, in such and such directions with such and such velocities. Then this last proposition is a *logical consequence* of the conjunction of the nomic, the occurrent, the dispositional, and the background premisses. That is to say, the combination of these premisses with the denial of the last proposition would be *logically inconsistent*. It is so in exactly the sense in which the combination of the premisses of a valid syllogism with the denial of its conclusion would be so.

THE NEGATIVE CONDITION

We can now work towards a definition of the statement that a certain event *e* was completely determined in respect of a certain characteristic. When we have defined this statement it will be easy to define the statement that a certain event was not completely determined in respect of a certain characteristic. I will begin with a concrete example, and will then generalize the result into a definition.

Suppose that a certain flash happened at a certain place and date. This will be a manifestation of a certain determinable characteristic, namely colour, in a certain perfectly determinate form. It may, for example, be a red flash of a certain perfectly determinate shade, intensity, and saturation. We may call shade, intensity, and saturation the three "dimensions" of colour, and we shall therefore symbolize the determinable characteristic colour by a three-suffix symbol C_{123}. When we want to symbolize a certain perfectly determinate value of this we shall use the symbol C_{123}^{abc}. This means that the shade has the determinate value a, that the intensity has the determinate value b, and that the saturation has the determinate value c. Each *index* indicates the determinate value which the dimension indicated by the corresponding *suffix* has in the given instance.

Now the statement that this flash was completely determined in respect of colour has the following meaning. It means that there is a set of true nomic, occurrent, dispositional, and background propositions which together entail the proposition that a manifestation of colour, of the precise shade, intensity, and saturation which this flash manifested, would happen at the place and time at which this flash happened. To say that this flash was *not* completely determined in respect of colour means that there is *no* set of true nomic, occurrent, dispositional, and background propositions which together entail the proposition that a manifestation of colour, of the precise shade, intensity, and saturation which this flash manifested, would happen at the place and time at which this flash happened.

There are two remarks to be made at this point. (i) It seems to me that the second statement is perfectly *intelligible,* even if no such statement be ever true. (ii) It is a purely *ontological* statement, and not in any way a statement about the limitations of our knowledge. Either there is such a set of true propositions, or there is not. There may be such a set, even if no one knows that there is; and there may be no such set, even if everyone believes that there is.

We can now give a general definition. The statement that a certain event e was completely determined in respect of a certain determinable characteristic C_{123} is equivalent to the conjunction of the following two propositions. (i) The event e was a manifestation of C_{123} in a certain perfectly determinate form C_{123}^{abc} at a certain place and date. (ii) There is a set of true nomic, occurrent, dispositional, and background propositions which together entail that a manifestation of C_{123} in the form C_{123}^{abc} would happen at the place and date at which e happened. The statement that e was *not* completely determined in respect of C_{123} is equivalent to the conjoint assertion of (i) and denial of (ii).

The next point to notice is that an event might be partly determined and partly undetermined in respect of a certain characteristic. As before, I will begin with a concrete example. Our flash might be completely determined in respect of shade and saturation, but not in respect of intensity. This would be equivalent to the conjunction of the following two statements. (i) That there is a set of true propositions, of the kind already mentioned, which together entail that a flash, of precisely the shade and saturation which this flash had, would happen at the place and date at which this flash happened. (ii) There is no such set of true propositions which together entail that a flash, of precisely the intensity which this flash had, would happen at the time and place at which this flash happened. We thus get the notion of "orders of indetermination" in respect of a given characteristic. If an event is undetermined in respect of one and only one dimension of a certain determinable characteristic, we say that it has "indetermination of the first order" in respect of this characteristic. If it is undetermined in respect of two and only two dimensions of a certain determinable characteristic, we say that it has "indetermination of the second order" in respect of this characteristic. And so on.

It is obvious that there is another possibility to be considered, which I will call "range of indetermination in respect of a given dimension of a given characteristic." Suppose that our flash is undetermined in respect of the intensity of its colour. There may be a set of true propositions, of the kind mentioned, which together entail that a flash, whose intensity falls within certain limits, would happen at the time and place at which this flash happened. This range of indetermination may be wide or narrow. Complete determination in respect of a given dimension of a given characteristic is the limiting case where the range of indetermination shuts up to zero about the actual value of this dimension for this event. Thus the "extent of indetermination" of an event with respect to a given characteristic depends in general upon two factors, namely (i) its order of indetermination with respect to the dimensions of this characteristic, and (ii) its range of indetermination with respect to those dimensions for which it is not completely determined.

We can now define the statement that a certain event e was completely determined. It means that e has zero range of indetermination for every dimension of every determinable characteristic of which it is a manifestation. The statement that a certain event e was *not* completely determined can now be defined. It means that e had a finite range of indetermination for at least one dimension of at least one of the characteristics of which it was a manifestation.

And now at last we can define "Determinism" and "Indeterminism." Determinism is the doctrine that *every* event is completely determined, in the sense just defined. Indeterminism, is the doctrine that some, and it may be all, events are not completely determined, in the sense defined. Both doctrines are, *prima facie,* intelligible, when defined as I have defined them.

There is one other point to be noticed. An event might be completely determined, and yet it might have a "causal ancestor" which was not completely determined. If Y is the total cause of Z, and X is the total cause of Y, I call both Y and X "causal ancestors" of Z.

Similarly, if W were the total cause of X, I should call Y, X, and W "causal ancestors" of Z. And so on. If at any stage in such a series there is a term, for example W, which contains a cause-factor that is not completely determined, the series will stop there, just as the series of human ancestors stops with Adam. Such a term may be called the "causal progenitor" of such a series. If Determinism be true, every event has causal ancestors, and therefore there are no causal progenitors. If Indeterminism be true, there are causal progenitors in the history of the world.

We can now state the negative condition which must be fulfilled if an action is to be categorically substitutable. Suppose that, at a certain time, an agent deliberated between two alternatives, A and B, and that he actually did A and not B. Suppose that the following conditions are fulfilled. (i) The doing of A by this agent at this moment was completely determined. (ii) The total cause of A being done contained as cause-factors a desire of a certain strength and persistence for A and a desire of a certain strength and persistence for B. (iii) These two desires were not completely determined in respect of strength and persistence. (iv) The range of indetermination was wide enough to include in it, as possible values, so strong and persistent a desire for B or so weak and fleeting a desire for A as would have determined the doing of B instead of the doing of A. Conditions (iii) and (iv) are the negative conditions which must be fulfilled if B is to be categorically substitutable for A. They amount to the following statement. It is consistent with (a) the laws of nature, including those of psychology, (b) the facts about the agent's dispositions and the dispositions of any other agent in the world at the moment of acting, (c) the facts about what was happening within and without the agent at that moment, and (d) the facts about the general background conditions at that moment, that the strength and persistence of the desires mentioned in (ii) should have any value that falls within the range mentioned in (iv).

Before we go further there is one point to be mentioned. Strictly speaking, what I have just stated are the negative conditions for *primary* categorical substitutability. For I have supposed the incomplete determination to occur at the *first* stage backwards, namely in one of the cause-factors in the total cause of the action A. It would be quite easy to define, in a similar way, the negative conditions for secondary, or tertiary, or any other order of categorical substitutability. All that is needed is that, at *some* stage in the causal ancestry of *A*, there shall be a total cause which contains as factors desires of the agent answering to the conditions which I have stated. That is to say, all that is necessary is that *A* shall have a causal ancestor which is a causal progenitor, containing as a factor an incompletely determined desire of the agent's.

We come now to the final question. Supposing that this negative condition were fulfilled, would this *suffice* to make an action categorically obligable? It seems to me plain that it would not. Unless some further and positive condition were fulfilled, all that one could say would be the following: "The desire to do *A* happened to be present in me with such strength and persistence, as compared with the desire to do *B*, that I did *A* and avoided *B*. The desire to do *B* might have happened to be present in me with such strength and persistence, as compared with the desire to do *A*, that I should have done *B* and avoided *A*." Now, if this is all, the fact that I did *A* and not *B* is, in the strictest sense, an *accident,* lucky or unlucky as the case may be. It may be welcomed or it may be deplored, but neither I nor anything else in the universe can properly be praised or blamed for it. It begins to look as if the categorical ought may be inapplicable, though for different reasons, both on the hypothesis that voluntary actions have causal progenitors and on the hypothesis that none of their causal ancestors are causal progenitors.

THE POSITIVE CONDITION

Let us now try to discover the positive conditions of categorical obligability. I think that we should naturally tend to answer the sort of objection which I have just raised in the following way. We should say: "I deliberately identified myself with my desire to do *A*, or I deliberately threw my weight on the side of that desire. I might instead have made no particular effort in one direction or the other; or I might have identified myself with, and thrown my weight on the side of, my desire to do *B*. So my desire to do *A* did not just happen to be present with the requisite strength and persistence, as compared with my desire to do *B*. It had this degree of strength and persistence because, and only because, I *reinforced* it by a deliberate effort, which I need not have made at all and which I could have made in favour of my desire to do *B*." Another way of expressing the same thing would be this: "I forced myself to do *A*; but I need not have done so, and, if I had not done so, I should have done *B*." Or again: "I might have forced myself to do *B*; but I did not, and so I did *A*."

It is quite plain that these phrases express a genuine positive experience with which we are all perfectly familiar. They are all, of course, metaphorical. It will be noticed that they all attempt to describe the generic fact by metaphors drawn from specific instances of it, for example, deliberately pressing down one scale of a balance, deliberately joining one side in a tug-of-war, deliberately thrusting a body in a certain direction against obstacles, and so on. In this respect they may be compared with attempts to describe the generic facts about time and change by metaphors drawn from specific instances, such as flowing streams, moving spots of light, and so on. The only use of such metaphors is to direct attention to the sort of fact which one wants one's hearers to contemplate. They give no help towards analysing or comprehending this fact. A metaphor helps us to understand a fact only when it brings out an analogy with a fact of a *different* kind, which we already understand. When a generic fact can be described only by metaphors drawn from specific instances of itself it is a sign that the fact is unique and peculiar, like the fact of temporal succession and the change of events from futurity, through presentness, to pastness.

Granted that there is this unique and peculiar factor of deliberate effort or reinforcement, how far does the recognition of it help us in our present problem? So far as I can see, it merely takes the problem one step further back. My doing of *A* is completely determined by a total cause which contains as factors my desire to do *A* and my desire to do *B*, each of which has a certain determinate strength and persistence. The preponderance of my desire to do *A* over my desire to do *B*, in respect of strength and persistence, is completely determined by a total cause which contains as a factor my putting forth a certain amount of effort to reinforce my desire for *A*. This effort-factor is not completely determined. It is logically consistent with all the nomic, occurrent, dispositional, and background facts that no effort should have been made, or that it should have been directed towards reinforcing the desire for *B* instead of the desire for *A*, or that it should have been put forth more or less strongly than it actually was in favour of the desire for *A*. Surely then we can say no more than it just happened to occur with a certain degree of intensity in favour of the desire for *A*.

I think that the safest course at this stage for those who maintain that some actions are categorically obligable would be the following. They should admit quite frankly what I have just stated, and should then say: "However paradoxical it may seem, we do regard ourselves and other people as morally responsible for accidents of this unique kind, and we do not regard them as morally responsible, in the categorical sense, for anything but such accidents and those consequences of them which would have been different if the accidents had happened differently. Only such accidents, and their causal descendants in the way of volition and action, are categorically obligable." If anyone should take up this position, I should not know how to refute him, though I should be strongly inclined to think him mistaken.

This is not, however, the position which persons who hold that some actions are categorically obligable generally do take at this point. I do not find that they ever state quite clearly what they think they believe, and I suspect that is because, if it were clearly stated, it would be seen to be impossible. I shall therefore try to state clearly what I think such people want to believe, and shall try to show that it is impossible. I suspect that they would quarrel with my statement that, on their view, the fact that one puts forth such and such an effort in support of a certain desire is, in the strictest sense, an accident. They would like to say that the putting forth of a certain amount of effort in a certain direction at a certain time *is* completely determined, but is determined in a unique and peculiar way. It is literally determined *by the agent or self,* considered as a substance or continuant, and not by a total cause which contains as factors *events in* and *dispositions of* the agent. If this could be maintained, our puttings-forth of effort would be completely determined, but their causes would neither be events nor contain events as cause-factors. Certain series of events would then originate from causal progenitors which are continuants and not events. Since the first event in such a series would be completely determined, it would not be an accident. And, since the total cause of such an event would not be an event and would not contain an event as a cause-factor, the two alternatives "completely determined" and "partially undetermined" would both be inapplicable to it. For these alternatives apply only to events.

I am fairly sure that this is the kind of proposition which people who profess to believe in Free Will want to believe. I have, of course, stated it with a regrettable crudity, of which they would be incapable. Now it seems to me clear that such a view is impossible. The putting-forth of an effort of a certain intensity, in a certain direction, at a certain moment, for a certain duration, is quite clearly an event or process, however unique and peculiar it may be in other respects. It is therefore subject to any conditions which self-evidently apply to every event, as such. Now it is surely quite evident that, if the beginning of a certain process at a certain time is determined at all, its total cause *must* contain as an essential factor another event or process which *enters into* the moment from which the determined event or process *issues*. I see no *prima facie* objection to there being events that are not completely determined. But, in so far as an event *is* determined, an essential factor in its total cause must be other *events*. How could an event possibly be determined to happen at a certain date if its total cause contained no factor to which the notion of date has any application? And how can the notion of date have any application to anything that is not an event?

Of course I am well aware that we constantly use phrases, describing causal transactions, in which a continuant is named as the cause and no event in that continuant is mentioned. Thus we say: "The stone broke the window," "The cat killed the mouse," and so on. But it is quite evident that all such phrases are elliptical. The first, for example, expresses what would be more fully expressed by the sentence: "The coming in contact of the moving stone with the window at a certain moment caused a process of disintegration to begin in the window at that moment." Thus the fact that we use and understand such phrases casts no doubt on the general principle which I have just enunciated.

Let us call the kind of causation which I have just described and rejected "non-occurrent causation of events." We will call the ordinary kind of causation, which I had in mind when I defined "Determinism" and "Indeterminism," "occurrent causation."

Now I think we can plausibly suggest what may have made some people think they believe that puttings-forth of effort are events which are determined by non-occurrent causation. It is quite usual to say that a man's putting-forth of effort in a certain direction on a certain occasion was determined by "Reason" or "Principle" or "Conscience" or "The Moral Law." Now these impressive names and phrases certainly do not denote events or even substances. If they denote anything, they stand for propositions or systems of propositions, or for those peculiar universals or systems of universals which Plato called "Ideas." If it were literally true that puttings-forth of effort are determined by such entities, we should have causation of events in time by timeless causes. But, of course, statements like "Smith's putting-forth of effort in a certain direction on a certain occasion was determined by the Moral Law" cannot be taken literally. The Moral Law, as such, has no causal efficacy. What is meant is that Smith's *belief* that a certain alternative would be in accordance with the Moral Law, and his *desire* to do what is right, were cause-factors in the total cause which determined his putting-forth of effort on the side of that alternative. Now this belief was an event, which happened when he began to reflect on the alternatives and to consider them in the light of the moral principles which he accepts and regards as relevant. And this desire was an event, which happened when his conative-emotional moral dispositions were stirred by the process of reflecting on the alternatives. Thus the use of phrases about action being "determined by the Moral Law" may have made some people think they believe that some events are determined by non-occurrent causation. But our analysis of the meaning of such phrases shows that the facts which they express give no logical support to this belief.

LIBERTARIANISM

We are now in a position to define what I will call "Libertarianism." This doctrine may be summed up in two propositions. (i) Some (and it may be all) voluntary actions have a causal ancestor which con-

tains as a cause-factor the putting-forth of an effort which is not completely determined in direction and intensity by occurrent causation.
(ii) In such cases the direction and the intensity of the effort are completely determined by nonoccurent causation, in which the self or
agent, taken as a substance or continuant, is the nonoccurent total
cause. Thus, Libertarianism, as defined by me, entails Indeterminism, as defined by me; but the converse does not hold.

If I am right, Libertarianism is self-evidently impossible, whilst
Indeterminism is *prima facie* possible. Hence, if categorical obligability entails Libertarianism, it is certain that no action can be
categorically obligable. But if categorical obligability entails only
Indeterminism, it is *prima facie* possible that some actions are categorically obligable. Unfortunately, it seems almost certain that categorical obligability entails more than Indeterminism, and it seems
very likely that it entails Libertarianism. It is therefore highly probable that the notion of categorical obligability is a delusive notion,
which neither has nor can have any application.

An Empirical Disproof
of Determinism?

~~~~~~

According to certain philosophers, the statement that a person could have done what he did not do lacks the proper epistemic credentials. The reason why this statement has been the bone of philosophical contention is its connection with the problem of free will and determinism.

It is usually held that a person acts of his own free will only if he could have acted otherwise. However, both libertarians and determinists have had their doubts about the epistemic qualifications of such statements. For example, Ledger Wood, a determinist, maintains that the statement that a person could have done otherwise is empirically meaningless. He says:

> . . . a careful analysis of the import of the retrospective judgement, "I could have acted otherwise than I did," will, I believe, disclose it to be an empirically meaningless statement.[1]

From the other side of the issue, William James, a libertarian, argues that science, and our knowledge of what has actually happened, cannot give us the least grain of information about what it was possible for a person to have done. He says:

* From *Freedom and Determinism*, Keith Lehrer, Editor. © Copyright 1966 by Random House, Inc. Reprinted by permission.
[1] Ledger Wood, "The Free Will Controversy," in Mandelbaum, Gramlich, and Anderson, eds., *Philosophic Problems* (New York: Macmillan, 1957), p. 308.

Science professes to draw no conclusions but such as are based on matters of fact, things that have actually happened; but how can any amount of assurance that something actually happened give us the least grain of information as to whether another thing might or might not have happened in its place? Only facts can be proved by other facts. With things that are possibilities and not facts, facts have no concern. If we have no other evidence than the evidence of existing facts, the possibility—question must remain a mystery never to be cleared up.[2]

Thus, both Wood and James, as well as others, think that it is impossible to know empirically that a person could have done other than he did do. I wish to show that this position is mistaken—that is, that it is possible to know empirically that a person could have done otherwise. I shall attempt to establish this, first by considering in general how we know what a person can do, and then by showing that skeptical doubt concerning our knowledge of what people can do is no better grounded than skeptical doubt concerning our knowledge of the color properties of unobserved objects. Finally, I wish to consider the implications of the possibility of such empirical knowledge for the problem of free will and determinism. I shall argue that it follows from the possibility of such knowledge that, if free will and determinism are not logically consistent, then we can know empirically that the principle of determinism is false. Subsequently, I shall consider the question of the consistency of free will and determinism.

I

I now wish to argue that we can know empirically that a person could have done otherwise.[3] A person could have done otherwise if he could have done what he did not do. Moreover, if it is true at

[2] William James, "The Dilemma of Determinism," in *Essays in Pragmatism* (New York: Hafner, 1955), p. 42.

[3] For the purpose of this paper, I shall assume that if a hypothesis is very highly probable with respect to some kind of empirical evidence, then it is possible to know that hypothesis empirically. Thus, I shall attempt to prove that the hypothesis that a person could have done otherwise is very highly probable with respect to some kind of empirical evidence. The line of argument I use was suggested by Richard Taylor, "I Can," in Sidney Morgenbesser and James Walsh, eds., *Free Will* (New Jersey: Prentice-Hall, 1962), p. 84.

the present time that a person can now do what he is not now doing, then, later, it will be true that he could have done something at this time which he did not do. This, of course, follows from the fact that "could" is sometimes merely the past indicative of "can." [4] What I now want to argue is that we do sometimes know empirically that a person can do at a certain time what he is not then doing, and, consequently, that he could have done at that time what he did not then do. Moreover, we can obtain empirical evidence in such a way that our methods will satisfy the most rigorous standards of scientific procedure.

I shall attempt to show that we can know empirically that a person could have done what he did not do by first considering the more general question of how we ever know what people can do. It is, I suppose, obvious that there is no problem of how we know a person can do something when we see him do it. In this case, the evidence that we have for the hypothesis that a person can do something entails the hypothesis. But all that is entailed by the evidence is that the person can do what we see him do *at the time we see him do it*. It is at least logically possible that he cannot do it at any other time. Thus, when we project the hypothesis that a person can do something at some time when we do not see him do it, the empirical evidence that we have for the hypothesis will not entail the hypothesis.

The problem of our knowledge of what people can do is, therefore, primarily the problem of showing how we know that people can do certain things at those times at which we do not see them do the things in question. The solution to the problem depends upon the recognition of the fact that one fundamental way (there are others) in which we know that a person can do something at some time when we do not see him do it is by seeing him do it at some other time. However, it is not merely a matter of seeing him do something at some other time that would justify our claim to know that he can do it at the time at which we do not see him do it, but of seeing him do it when certain other epistemic conditions are also satisfied. I shall discuss four such conditions, which seem to me to be the most important. I shall call them the conditions of *temporal*

---

[4] See J. L. Austin, "Ifs and Cans," in J. O. Urmson and G. J. Warnock, eds., *Philosophical Papers* (London: Oxford University Press, 1961), p. 163.

propinquity, circumstantial variety, agent similarity, and simple frequency.

TEMPORAL PROPINQUITY   The amount of time that has elapsed between the time at which we see a person perform an action and the time at which it is claimed that he can perform the action is of considerable importance. For example, if I saw a man perform forty push-ups twenty years ago and have not seen him do it since, that would hardly justify my claim to know that he can do it now. On the other hand, if I saw him do it yesterday, my claim would have much greater merit. The less time that elapses between the time at which we see a person perform an action and the time at which we claim to know that he can perform it, the more justified our claim. This condition requires one qualification.[5] Certain actions—for example, running a four-minute mile—require unusual endurance; consequently, if we have just seen a person do such a thing, it is a good guess that, being tired, he cannot do it now. The condition is relevant even in the case of such actions, but we must add the qualification that sufficient time has elapsed between the time at which we saw the person perform the action and the time at which it is claimed that he could have performed the action, so that the effects of fatigue would not prevent or hinder the person from performing it.

CIRCUMSTANTIAL VARIETY   The greater the variety of circumstances under which we have seen the person perform an action, the more justified we are in claiming to know that he can perform it. There is also a qualification needed here. Sometimes, though we have not seen a person perform an action in a very great variety of circumstances, we have seen him perform the action under circumstances very similar to the circumstances he is in when it is claimed that he can perform it. In this case, the greater the similarity of the circumstances, the better the evidence.

AGENT SIMILARITY   If the condition of the agent changes radically, from the time at which we see him perform an action to the time at which it is claimed that he can perform it, then our evidence

---

[5] Compare P. H. Nowell-Smith, "Ifs and Cans," in *Theoria*, XXVI, 96–97.

that he can peform the action may be greatly weakened. For example, if we see a man lift a two-hundred-pound weight, and he subsequently breaks his arm, our having seen him lift the weight is surely not very good evidence that he can do it now that his arm is broken. Thus, the greater the similarity of the condition of the agent, at the time when we see him perform the action, to the condition of the agent at the time at which we claim that he can perform it, the greater the justification of our claim. To some extent this condition, like the preceding one, may be formulated as a condition of variety rather than as a condition of similarity. That is, if we have seen the agent perform an action at times when his condition has varied greatly, then, even though the condition of the agent at the time at which it is claimed that he can perform the action is quite different from what it was when we saw him perform it, the claim might, nevertheless, be fairly well justified. However, it seems to me that with respect to the circumstances, variety is more important, while, with respect to the condition of the agent, similarity is more important. The reason for this is that great changes in circumstances are often unimportant, while small changes in the condition of the agent may often be crucial.

SIMPLE FREQUENCY Other conditions aside, the more frequently we have seen a person perform an action, the more justified we are in claiming to know that he can perform the action when we do not see him perform it.

These conditions are related in various ways. For example, temporal propinquity tends to produce agent similarity, because generally people change less in a shorter time than in a longer time. Of course, circumstantial variety contributes to simple frequency, and vice versa. Thus, these conditions, which are simple canons of inductive evidence for a certain sort of hypothesis, are inductively interdependent.

Moreover, the importance of the various conditions depends to a considerable extent upon the kind of action involved. With respect to actions that one usually retains the ability to perform for a long time, such as wiggling one's ears, the condition of temporal propinquity is less important, whereas with respect to actions that one quickly loses the ability to perform, such as running a four-minute mile, the condition of temporal propinquity is much more important.

However, if all of these conditions are very well satisfied with respect to any action, we possess sufficient empirical evidence to support the hypothesis that a person can perform the action when we do not see him perform it, and, in the absence of any evidence to the contrary, we are certainly justified in claiming to know that the hypothesis is true. Indeed, these conditions are typical of the usual canons of inductive evidence; if they are satisfied, then, by the usual canons of inductive evidence, our evidence is excellent.

II

It will not be difficult to imagine an experiment, which we could quite easily carry out, that would enable us to obtain such evidence. To avoid unnecessary complications, we shall concern ourselves with one very simple action, the lifting of an arm. Now let us imagine that we find a subject who is normal in every way, and fabricate an experiment to investigate when our subject can, and when he cannot, perform this very simple action. For example, we might first instruct him to lift his arm whenever we tell him to, and see that he does this. We might then instruct him to lift his arm whenever we tell him not to, and see that he does this. We might then tell him to heed or not to heed our instructions, as he wishes, and see that he sometimes lifts his arm when we tell him to, and sometimes does not, and that he sometimes lifts his arm when we tell him not to, and sometimes does not. We might then run this same experiment under a variety of circumstances, indoors and outdoors, under stress and under relaxed conditions, with a weight attached to his arm and without impediments, and so forth. Moreover, we might keep careful records of the condition of the subject throughout all our experiments, and, finally, we might vary the condition of the subject by the use of drugs, hypnotism, and so forth.

Now, suppose that we instruct our subject to heed or not heed our instructions as he wishes, and insure that the condition of the subject, as well as the circumstances in which he is placed, are those we have found to be most propitious for arm-lifting. Moreover, suppose that we watch him lift his arm, then avert our eyes for a moment, and, subsequently, see him lift his arm again. In this case, the conditions of temporal propinquity, circumstantial variety, agent similarity, and simple frequency would certainly be satisfied.

Consequently, we would then have sufficient empirical evidence to support the hypothesis that the agent could have lifted his arm during that brief period when we did not see him lift his arm, and, consequently, we would be justified in claiming to know that the hypothesis is true.

Furthermore, this claim would be justified whether or not the agent lifted his arm at the time in question, and, indeed, would be justified even if we knew that he did not lift it. In fact, even if we do not avert our eyes but see that he does not move his arm at the time in question, this in no way detracts from the value of our evidence. Under the conditions we have imagined, the fact that our subject does not lift his arm need provide no evidence whatever to support the hypothesis that he cannot lift it.

The latter claim is surely the crux of the matter. To see that it is justified, let us suppose that we know from what the agent tells us that he did not try or make any attempt to lift his arm. The relevance of such knowledge is this. If the agent tried and failed, that would be evidence that he could not perform the action, but there is a great difference between failing when one has tried and mere nonperformance. If we are able to rule out the hypothesis that the agent tried and failed, and if the condition of the agent as well as the circumstances in which he is placed are those we have found to be most favorable for arm-lifting, then the mere fact that he does not lift his arm would not support the hypothesis that he cannot lift it.

An analogy should help to clarify this point. Suppose that a car is tuned and checked so that it is in perfect operating condition and is then placed in circumstances that most favor good performance. If someone tries to start the car, turns the key, sets the choke, and so forth, and the car fails to start, this is evidence that it cannot start. On the other hand, if no attempt is made to start the car, then the mere fact that the car does not start in no way supports the hypothesis that it cannot start.

Therefore, if we know from our experiment: (i) that the condition of the agent and the circumstances in which we have placed him are ideal for arm-lifting, and (ii) that his not lifting his arm provides no evidence that he cannot lift it, then our experimental empirical evidence is sufficient to justify our claim to know that the agent could have lifted his arm at a time when he did not lift it.

Since there is no impossibility of any sort involved in our imaginary experiment, there being no logical difficulty involved in actually carrying it out, it follows that it is possible to know empirically that a person could have done otherwise. It seems altogether reasonable to suppose that, were the experiment actually carried out, the results would be approximately what we have imagined them to be. Moreover, the uncontrolled but abundant evidence of everyday life also clearly provides us with empirical evidence sufficient to justify our claim to know empirically that a person could have done otherwise. Indeed, the experiment I have asked you to imagine is not *necessary* for the attainment of such knowledge, but it is *sufficient,* and that is the point at issue.

III

At this point, I wish to consider several objections that might be raised against the preceding argument. In the first place, it might be objected that the empirical evidence that we would obtain from our imaginary experiment would not establish categorically that the agent could have done otherwise, but would rather establish hypothetically only that the agent could have done otherwise, *if* certain conditions had been different.[6] However, the experiment would establish *both* that, at certain times, the subject could have done otherwise, if certain conditions had been different, *and* that, at other times, the subject could have done otherwise, had the conditions been precisely as they were. It is most important not to obliterate this distinction. For example, we might discover that, when our subject is hypnotized and given certain instructions, he can lift his arm only when he is told to. In such a case, if he does not lift his arm, we would only be justified in asserting hypothetically that he could have lifted his arm if we had told him to. Or, suppose that we instruct him, again under hypnotic control, to lift

---

[6] Compare P. H. Nowell-Smith, *Ethics* (Oxford: Basil Blackwell, 1957), pp. 240–41.

his arm only *if* he has decided to do so five minutes earlier. In this situation, if the subject does not lift his arm, we would only be justified in asserting hypothetically that he could have lifted his arm, *if* he had decided to five minutes earlier. However, if we have just seen him lift his arm under the most favorable cricumstances, and, without the conditions being altered in any way, he does not lift his arm now, we would be justified in asserting categorically that he could have lifted his arm—and no *ifs* about it.

IV

Next I wish to consider the most skeptical objections that can be raised against what I have said concerning our knowledge of what people can do. A defender of the view that it is impossible to know empirically that a person could have done otherwise might contend that it is possible to know that a person can do something only when we see him do it. Thus, when we do not see a person do something, it is impossible to know empirically that he can do it then. Since we never see a person do what he does not do, it is impossible to know empirically that a person can do what he does not do. Formulated in this way, the objection has, I believe, little to recommend it.

In the first place, it amounts to the view that no amount of evidence is sufficient to justify our claim to know that a person can do something, if the evidence does not entail that he can do it. For, the evidence of seeing a person do something entails that he can do it, and, according to this objection, it is the only evidence that makes knowledge possible. Thus, no amount of inductive evidence that does not entail its conclusion would justify our claim to knowledge. Moreover, this view has the consequence that we cannot even know empirically that a person can do what he does do, when we do not see him do it. This is surely absurd. Whatever skeptical doubts one might entertain concerning the possibility of knowing empirically that a person can do what he does not do, it is obvious that it is sometimes possible to know empirically that a person can do what he does do, even though we do not see him do it. For example, if we see a man standing with his finger on the only button attached to a bell, and we hear the bell ring, then we know empirically that the man can push the button, even if we did not see him push it.

However, the objection may be reformulated so that it does not have the consequence just mentioned. It could be argued that it is only in those cases in which a person does not do something that it is impossible to know empirically that he can do it. The grounds for this contention might simply be that, while it is at least logically possible to see a person do what he does, and, consequently, possible to know empirically that he can do it, it is logically impossible to see a person do what he does not do, and, consequently, impossible to know empirically that the person can do it. This formulation does not have the consequence that only evidence entailing that a person can do something would justify our claim to know that he can do it. However, it does have the consequence that it is only possible to obtain evidence that would justify our claim to know that a person can do something, if it is possible to obtain evidence entailing that he can do it. For, seeing a person do something entails that he can do it, and, according to this formulation, it is possible to know empirically that a person can do something only if it is possible to see him do it.

Even though this formulation of the objection does not have the consequences of the earlier formulation, it embodies a kind of skepticism that is no more justified than, for example, skepticism concerning our knowledge of the color of objects. Indeed, a very close epistemological analogy can be drawn between these cases. In the first place, just as it is possible to obtain evidence that entails that a person can do something by seeing him do it, so it is possible to obtain evidence that entails that an object is a certain color by seeing that it is that color. Moreover, just as it is logically possible to obtain such evidence that a person can do something he did do, even though we did not in fact see him do it, so it is logically possible to obtain such evidence that an object is a certain color, though we did not in fact see it. Finally, just as it is logically impossible to see a person do something he does not do, and consequently, impossible to obtain evidence that entails that he can do it, so it is logically impossible to see that an object is a certain color when it is unseen, and consequently, impossible to obtain evidence that entails that it is that color. Therefore, there is, I believe, no more justification for skepticism concerning our knowledge of what a person can do when he is not doing it than there is for skepticism concerning our knowledge of what color an object is, when it is unseen.[7] With that claim, I rest the case.

V

Now that we have shown that it is possible to know empirically that a person could have done otherwise, it will be useful to see why anyone should wish to deny this. For there is, I believe, at least one very interesting reason for doing so. It is this. The principle of determinism, stated in its simplest form, is the principle that whatever happens is caused. It follows from this that whatever a person does, that being something that happens, is caused. Moreover, if something is caused, then, given the conditions that caused it, whatever happens, *could* not have happened otherwise. Thus, if determinism is true, and, consequently, whatever a person does is caused, then, given the conditions that caused it, things could not have happened otherwise. It follows from this that the person could not have done otherwise. So, if what a person does is caused, then he could not have done otherwise. Therefore, if it is possible to know empirically that a person could have done otherwise, then it is possible to know empirically that what he did was not caused. Moreover, it has seemed to many philosophers, for reasons I shall discuss later, that it is impossible to know empirically that what a person did was *not* caused, and they have concluded that it is impossible to know empirically that a person could have done otherwise.

I have argued, contrary to what is here concluded, that it is possible to know empirically that a person could have done otherwise. What we must now decide is whether it follows from this, as the line of thought sketched above suggests, that it is possible to know empirically that what a person did was uncaused. I now wish to consider two objections that may be raised against that line of thought.

[7] Nowell-Smith defends a similar position in *Ethics,* pp. 241–43.

VI

In the first place, it may be objected that it does not follow from the statement that something is caused that whatever happens could not have happened otherwise. For example, John Stuart Mill argued that causes do not *necessitate*, that to say that something is caused is not to say that it *must* happen but only that it *will* happen.[8] It would be a logical corollary of this thesis that to say that something is caused is not to say that things *could not* happen otherwise, but only that they *will not* happen otherwise. However, it is interesting to notice that not even Mill was quite able to maintain this position consistently. At one point we find him saying:

> That whatever happens, could not have happened otherwise, unless something had taken place which was capable of preventing it, no one surely needs hesitate to admit.[9]

Of course, he then goes on to qualify what he has just said. He says:

> But to call this by the name of Necessity is to use the term in a sense so different from its primitive and familiar meaning, from that which it bears in the common occasions of life, as to amount almost to a play upon words.[10]

It is hard to see how this helps. Whether we call the former by the name of Necessity or not, it amounts simply to the principle that whatever happens could not have happened otherwise. Indeed, the phrase, "unless something had taken place which was capable of preventing it," is really redundant. So, even Mill here concedes that if whatever happens is caused, then whatever happens could not have happened otherwise.

Moreover, this is something that ought to be conceded. Even if it is the case that, in some ordinary sense of the word "cause," to say that something is caused does not entail that what happened could not have happened otherwise, it is also the case that, in another perfectly familiar sense of the word "cause," to say that some-

[8] John Stuart Mill, *A System of Logic* (London: Longmans, Green and Co., 1936), p. 549.
[9] *Ibid.*
[10] *Ibid.*

thing is caused does entail that what happened could not have happened otherwise. For example, if a brick has been dropped from a fifty-story building and there is nothing to prevent it from falling toward the ground, it is surely the case that certain natural forces will cause the brick to fall toward the ground, and it is surely also the case, not only that the brick will not do otherwise, but also that it could not do otherwise. Moreover, the example will not be altered in any relevant respect if we substitute a man for a brick.

Thus, as Mill recognizes, there is a sense of the word "cause," in which to say that whatever happens is caused commits one to the thesis that whatever happens could not have happened otherwise.

VII

The second objection is, I believe, of much greater importance. It may be objected that the sense of the word "could" that is involved when we say of a man that he could have done otherwise, implying that he has free will, is quite different from that sense of the word "could" that is involved when we say that he could not have done otherwise, implying that his action was caused. For example, G. E. Moore remarked:

> All that is certain about the matter is: (1) that, if we have Free Will, it must be true, in *some* sense, that we sometimes *could* have done what we did not do; (2) that, if everything is caused, it must be true, in *some* sense, that we *never could* have done, what we did not do. What is very *un*certain, and what certainly needs to be investigated, is whether these two meanings of the word "could" are the same.[11]

(I assume that the sense of "could" that is involved when we say of our experimental subject that he could have done otherwise is that sense of "could" that is related to free will, for a person acts of his own free will only if he could have done otherwise in this sense of "could.")

The really crucial question to be answered here is the following: Is it logically consistent to say both that a person could have done

---

[11] G. E. Moore, *Ethics* (London: Oxford University Press, 1955), p. 131.

otherwise, in the sense of "could" related to free will, *and* that he could not have done otherwise, in the sense of "could" related to causation? The reason why this question is crucial is that if the answer to the question is negative, then free will and determinism are logically inconsistent, even if the two senses of "could" mentioned above are quite different. Moreover, if the answer to the question is negative, and free will and determinism are inconsistent, then the argument that I presented earlier would prove that we can know empirically that the thesis of determinism is false.

In order to clarify this question, and to avoid ambiguity, let us introduce a technical term, "causally possible," to use in place of "could," where the latter would be used in connection with causation. Hereafter, the term "could" will be used in the sense related to free will. This innovation will not beg the question at issue, for we need not make any assumptions concerning the semantical or logical relations between "could" and "causally possible."

We may gain something further in clarity by defining "causally possible" in terms of "cause." Let us say that it is causally impossible for something to happen if and only if there exist antecedent conditions sufficient to cause it not to happen, and that it is causally impossible for something not to happen if and only if there exist antecedent conditions sufficient to cause it to happen. Something is causally possible if and only if it is not causally impossible. We may then say that something is causally determined if and only if it is causally impossible for it not to happen. The thesis of determinism then becomes the thesis that whatever happens, happens under conditions such that it was causally impossible for it not to happen.

In this terminology, the crucial question is this: Is it logically consistent to say both that a person could have done otherwise and that it was causally impossible for him to have done otherwise? Or, to put the same question in the present tense: Is it logically consistent to say both that a person can do otherwise and that it is causally impossible for him to do otherwise? It is easy to see that if the answer to these questions is negative, then free will and determinism are inconsistent. For, if determinism is true, then, whatever a person does, it is causally impossible for him to do otherwise. On the other hand, if a person acts of his own free will, then he can do otherwise. Therefore, to prove the consistency of free will and determinism, we must prove the following thesis: It is logically consistent to say both that a person can do something and that it is causally impossible for him to do it. I now wish to examine the merits of this thesis, which I shall refer to hereafter as the "consistency thesis."

VIII

One traditional defense of the consistency thesis is based on the idea that statements asserting that a person can do something are analyzable as causal conditionals, which assert that he will do it if certain specified conditions are fulfilled. This line of argument, which I now wish to examine in some detail, has recently been criticized by J. L. Austin, on the grounds that the if-statements proposed as analyses are not causal conditionals.

It has been argued that "I can" is analyzable as "I shall if I choose." Austin gives the following arument to show that "I shall if I choose" is not a conditional statement.

> And now for something about "I *shall* if I choose"—what sort of *if* have we here? The point to notice is, that "I shall" is not an assertion of *fact* but an expression of *intention* verging towards the giving of some undertaking, and the *if*, consequently, is the *if* not of condition but of *stipulation*. In sentences like:
>
> > I shall marry him if I choose,
> > I intend to marry him if I choose,
> > I promise to marry him if he will have me,
>
> the *if*-clause is a part of the object phrase governed by the initial verb ("shall," "intend," "promise"), if this is an allowable way of putting it; or again, the *if* qualifies the *content* of the undertaking given, or of the intention announced, it does *not* qualify the giving of the undertaking.[12]

These remarks are, I believe, completely in error. "I shall if I choose" is simply not used to express any intention whatsoever, with or without stipulations. Expressions of the form "I shall . . . if—" do sometimes express an intention to do something with a cer-

---

[12] Austin, "Ifs and Cans," p. 162.

tain stipulation. For example, "I shall buy a boat if I get a raise" expresses my intention to buy a boat, with the stipulation that I get a raise.

But "I shall if I choose" is not typically used in this way. This expression is used in a context in which there is some doubt about whether the speaker has any choice, and by saying, "I shall if I choose," the speaker is in effect saying, "The choice is mine." For example, consider the sentence suggested by Austin, "I shall marry him if I choose." In what circumstances would it be natural to say that? Well, a woman might say that, if someone were implying that she would find it difficult to marry a certain man, or if someone were suggesting that perhaps he would not marry her. By saying, "I shall marry him if I choose," she would in effect be saying, "The choice is *mine!*" Notice that there is no reason to say that the speaker has expressed any intention whatsoever. Indeed, it would be most peculiar to suggest that by saying, "I shall marry him if I choose," she has expressed her intention to marry him with the stipulation that she chooses!

Thus, these remarks of Austin's, since they are mistaken, do not prove that "I shall if I choose" is not a conditional. Moreover, even if "I shall if I choose" is not a conditional, that would not show that the consistency thesis is false. For, as I now propose to show, if the statement that a person can do something is logically equivalent to, or entailed by, any causal conditional asserting that he will do it if certain conditions are fulfilled, then it follows that the consistency thesis is true.

IX

To prove the consistency thesis, it must be shown that the statement that a person can do something is logically consistent with the statement that is causally impossible for him to do it. Thus, it must be shown that such a statement as

(1) Smith can move

is logically consistent with the statement

(2) It is causally impossible for Smith to move.

It is true that if (1) were equivalent to some causal conditional of the form "Smith will move if . . . ," then (1) could be shown to be consistent with (2). For example, suppose the statement

(3) Smith will move if he believes it is in his best interests

to be a causal conditional. It is consistent with

(2) It is causally impossible for Smith to move.

Supposing (3) to be a causal conditional, it simply asserts that Smith's believing that it will be in his best interests to move (together with other conditions that are presupposed) will be a condition sufficient to cause Smith to move. It is obvious that these two statements are consistent. No contradiction follows from (3) and (2); what follows is that it is not the case that Smith believes that it will be in his best interests to move.

Thus, if

(1) Smith can move

were equivalent to

(3) Smith will move if he believes it is in his best interests,

then (1) would be consistent with

(2) It is causally impossible for Smith to move,

because (3) is consistent with (2). Obviously, if two statements are equivalent, then they are consistent with the same statements.

Moreover, if (1) were entailed by, though not equivalent to (3), it would still follow that (1) is consistent with (2). For let us suppose that

(3) Smith will move if he believes it is in his best interests,

being a causal conditional, entailed

(1) Smith can move.

We have already seen that (3) is consistent with

(2) It is causally impossible for Smith to move,

and it follows from this that (1) is consistent with (2). For if a statement P entails a statement Q, and P is consistent with a statement R, then Q is also consistent with R.

On the other hand, if (1) entailed (3) but was not logically equivalent to (3), it would not follow from this that (1) is consistent with (2).

The conclusion that a statement P is consistent with a statement R does not follow from the premise that P entails a statement Q that is consistent with R. This can easily be seen by reflecting on the following counterexample. The statement

(p) Pennies are copper and dimes are silver

entails

(q) Dimes are silver,

which is consistent with

(r) Pennies are not copper.

Though (p) entails (q), and (q) is consistent with (r), (p) is obviously inconsistent with (r).

Therefore, we may conclude that, if it were shown that the statement that a person can do something is equivalent to or entailed by a causal conditional which asserts that he will do it if certain conditions are satisfied, that would prove the consistency thesis. But the thesis would not be proven by showing that the statement that a person can do something entails a causal conditional of that sort.

X

However, I shall now argue that the statement that a person can do something is not entailed by, and hence not equivalent to, any causal conditional which asserts that he will do it if certain conditions are fulfilled. Let us consider a somewhat different conditional. The conditional

(5) Smith will move if he is not chained

clearly does not entail

(1) Smith can move.

It would be easy to think of situations in which (5) would be true and (1) false—for example, one in which Smith wants very much to move but cannot do so because he is chained.

Thus, (5) is compatible with both

> (6) Smith cannot move if he is chained

and

> (7) Smith is chained.

But (6) and (7) entail the denial of (1)—namely, that Smith can move.

Though this argument only shows that (5) does not entail (1), and apparently leaves open the possibility that (1) is entailed by some other causal conditional, the argument can be extended to the general case. For if a statement of the form

> (5′) S will do X if condition C obtains

is a causal conditional, then it will be compatible with both

> (6′) S cannot do X if condition C does not obtain

and

> (7′) Condition C does not obtain.

For it is logically possible that some condition which is a sufficient condition to cause a person to do something should also be a necessary condition of his being able to do it and that the condition should fail to occur. But (6′) and (7′) entail

> (8′) S cannot do X,

and since (5′), (6′), and (7′) are jointly compatible, they do not entail

> (1′) S can do X.

Consequently, (5′) does not entail (1′). For if a conjunction of statements P, Q, and R is consistent and entails a statement S, then, obviously, none of the statements entails the denial of S. Therefore, "S can do X" is not entailed by any causal conditional of the form "S will do X if. . . ."

We have now seen that the statement that a person can do something is not entailed by, and hence not equivalent to, any causal conditional asserting that he will do it if certain conditions are satisfied. Of course, it follows from this that the statement that a person can do something is not analyzable in terms of any causal conditional of that sort. Therefore, the consistency thesis cannot be proven by showing that the statement that a person can do something stands in any of these logical relationships to such causal conditionals.

XI

So far, we have not found any reason for thinking that the statement that a person could have done otherwise is consistent with the statement that his behavior was causally determined. Should we then conclude that the two statements are inconsistent? In that case, we should have to accept the conclusion that we can know empirically that a person's behavior was not causally determined, and, therefore, that the thesis of determinism is false. For we have already shown that we can know empirically that a person could have done otherwise.

It is sometimes thought that there are quite conclusive grounds for believing that we cannot know empirically that *anything* is uncaused. For example, we find G. J. Warnock saying:

> . . . there could never occur any event which it would be neccessary, or even natural, to describe as an uncaused event. It could never be said that among its complex and indefinitely numerous antecedents *none* could be said to be sufficient for its occurrence. And this is to say that nothing could occur which would require us to hold that S (the principle of determinism) is false. . . . It calls for no supporting empirical evidence, for none could count against it. It cannot be empirically tested, for no test could fail—or rather nothing could be made to count as a test.[18]

This familiar line of thought seems to me to have little merit. It is true that no matter how long we search for and fail to find the cause of some event, the logical possibility always remains that the event has a cause. So Warnock is right when he says that it would never be *necessary* to describe an event as uncaused. But it hardly follows from this that no empirical evidence can count against the hypothesis that an event is caused or in favor of the

[18] G. J. Warnock, "Every Event Has a Cause," in Anthony Flew, ed., *Logic and Language,* Second Series (Oxford: Basil Blackwell, 1959), pp. 106–7.

hypothesis that it is uncaused. Indeed, all the argument shows is that no amount of empirical evidence would *entail* that an event is uncaused, and, consequently, it fails to show that no amount of empirical evidence would be sufficient to establish inductively that an event is uncaused.

For, in the first place, all genuinely universal hypotheses are such that no amount of empirical evidence would entail that they are true, but surely this does not prove that such hypotheses cannot be inductively established. Moreover, to take a more exact analogy, no matter how long we search for and fail to find a natural solvent for a particular substance, the logical possibility always remains that it has a natural solvent, but this does not prove that we cannot inductively establish that the substance has no natural solvent. It is perfectly possible that empirical evidence should inductively establish that no mule is fertile, that some particular substance has no solvent, or that an event has no cause, even though the evidence leaves open the logical possibility that there are fertile mules, that the substance in question does have a solvent, and that the event has a cause.

XII

Thus, it may be that some empirical evidence could establish the falsity of determinism. However, it is incongruous to suppose that the *kind* of evidence we would obtain in our imaginary experiment to support the hypothesis that the subject could have done otherwise would disprove the thesis of determinism. If we know from our experiment that the condition of the subject and the circumstances in which we have placed him are ideal for arm-lifting, then, when his arm remains unmoved, our experimental evidence is sufficient to justify the hypothesis that the subject could have done otherwise. But this evidence hardly seems sufficient to justify the hypothesis that his behavior was not causally determined! To put the matter another way, the experimental evidence that renders highly probable the hypothesis that the subject could have done otherwise fails to render highly probable the hypothesis that his behavior was not causally determined.

This fact provides the basis for a proof that the statement that a person could have done otherwise is consistent with the statement that his behavior was causally determined. It is a theorem of the calculus of probability, which follows from the most evident axioms, that if one hypothesis entails another hypothesis, then any evidence that renders the first hypothesis probable to a certain degree renders the second hypothesis probable to at least that degree.[14] It is a corollary of this theorem that if one hypothesis is rendered highly probable by some evidence that does not render a second hypothesis highly probable, then the first hypothesis does not entail the second.

This corollary applies to our present argument in the following way. We have said that our experimental evidence renders highly probable the hypothesis that our subject could have done otherwise. On the other hand, we have said the evidence fails to render highly probable the hypothesis that his behavior was not causally determined. It follows from these facts, together with the corollary, that the hypothesis that our subject could have done otherwise does not entail the hypothesis that his behavior was not causally determined. From this it follows that the statement that a person could have done otherwise is logically consistent with the statement that his behavior was causally determined.

XIII

It is tempting to conclude from this that the statement that a person could have done otherwise is logically consistent with the thesis of determinism, and, consequently, that we need not concede that our evidence for the former statement proves that the thesis of determinism is false. But this conclusion does not quite follow. The thesis of determinism not only implies that a person's behavior is determined, it also implies that the conditions that determined his

---

[14] See any standard treatise on probability. For example, Hans Reichenbach, *The Theory of Probability* (Los Angeles: University of California Press, 1949), pp. 54–59; or Rudolph Carnap, *Logical Foundations of Probability* (Chicago: University of Chicago Press, 1950), pp. 285–87. The axioms in question are the following: (i) $1 \geqq P(h, e) \geqq o$; (ii) $P(h, e) + P(\text{not-}h, e) = 1$, if e is consistent; and (iii) $P(h \text{ or } k, e) = P(h, e) + P(k, e)$, if h and k are mutually exclusive. A related theorem is proved in my article, "Doing the Impossible," *Australasian Journal of Philosophy*, XLII (1964), 97. However, there is a misprint in the proof. Proposition P7 in the proof should read: $P(h \text{ or not-}h', e) = P(h, e) + P(\text{not-}h', e)$.

behavior were determined, that the conditions that determined those conditions were determined, and so forth. When a person's behavior is determined, and the conditions that determine his behavior are determined, and so forth, let us say that his behavior is *ancestorially* determined. (This term is chosen because, if a person's behavior is ancestorially determined, then all the causal ancestors of his behavior have causal ancestors.)

Thus, it is a consequence of determinism, not only that a person's behavior is causally determined, but also that it is ancestorially determined. However, given the temporal character of the causal relation, it follows from the fact that a person's behavior is ancestorially determined that the causal ancestry, the chain of causal determination, of his behavior extends backward in time to conditions that existed before he was born. Moreover, given the principle of the transitivity of causal determination—that is, the principle that if A is causally determined by B and B is causally determined by C, then A is causally determined by C—it follows from the fact that a person's behavior is ancestorially determined that his behavior is causally determined by conditions that existed before he was born, and, consequently, by conditions over which he had no control.[15]

The question we must now answer is this: Is the statement that a person could have done otherwise logically consistent with the statement that his behavior was ancestorially determined? If the answer is negative, then we must accept the conclusion that our evidence for the former statement proves that a person's behavior is not ancestorially determined and, therefore, that the thesis of determinism is false. However, we need not accept that conclusion. An affirmative answer to the question may be established by modifying an argument previously presented.

Let us again consider the experimental evidence, which renders highly probable the hypothesis that our subject could have done otherwise. Just as that evidence fails to render highly probable the hypothesis that our subject's behavior was not causally determined,

---

[15] This point was suggested to me by Professor Taylor's comment on an earlier paper of mine. My paper, "Doing the Impossible," and his comments, "Not Trying to do the Impossible," *Australasian Journal of Philosophy*, XLII (1964), pp. 98–100, are printed together. For my reply see "Doing the Impossible: A Second Try," *Australasian Journal of Philosophy*, XLII (1964), 249–51.

so it fails to render highly probable the hypothesis that his behavior was not ancestorially determined. For the evidence would hardly justify the hypothesis that our subject's behavior was not causally determined, or the hypothesis that the conditions that determined these conditions were not causally determined, or that the conditions that determined those conditions were not causally determined, and so forth. Nor, for that matter, would the evidence justify the hypothesis that any of these conditions were not causally determined. Consequently, the evidence fails to render highly probable the hypothesis that our subject's behavior was not ancestorially determined.

Of course, it follows from the corollary mentioned together with these facts that the hypothesis that the subject could have done otherwise does not entail the hypothesis that his behavior was not ancestorially determined. It follows from this that the statement that a person could have done otherwise is logically consistent with the statement that his behavior was ancestorially determined. We may conclude, then, that the statement that a person could have done otherwise is logically consistent with the thesis of determinism. Finally, we may with perfect consistency *both* concede that the empirical evidence described earlier justifies our claim to know that a person could have done otherwise *and* deny that the evidence justifies the claim to know that the thesis of determinism is false.

J. J. C. SMART

Free Will, Praise and Blame

~~~~~~

In this article I try to refute the so-called "libertarian" theory of free will, and to examine how our conclusions ought to modify our common attitudes of praise and blame. In attacking the libertarian view, I shall try to show that it cannot be consistently stated. That is, my discussion will be an "analytic-philosophical" one. I shall neglect what I think is in practice an equally powerful method of attack on the libertarian: a challenge to state his theory in such a way that it will fit in with modern biology and psychology, which are becoming increasingly physicalistic.

It is difficult to state clearly just what is the metaphysical view about free will to which I object. This is because it seems to me to be a self-contradictory one, and in formal logic any proposition whatever can be shown to follow from a contradiction. However in practice a confused and contradictory view does lead to a certain fairly characteristic set of propositions and attitudes. (In the case we are considering, one of these is that righteous indignation is an appropriate emotion in certain circumstances.[1]) The reason why a contradictory position can in practice lead to a circumscribed set of

---

* From J. J. C. Smart, "Free Will, Praise and Blame," *Mind*, *LXX*, No. 279 (July, 1961), 291–306. Reprinted by permission of the author and the editor of *Mind*.
[1] See Paul Edwards, "Hard and soft determinism," and John Hospers, "What means this freedom?" in Sydney Hook, ed., *Determinism and Freedom in the Age of Modern Science* (New York: New York University Press, 1958), pp. 104–13 and 113–30.

propositions is that the contradiction is not recognised by those who hold the views in question. Hence the logical proof schema which enables you to deduce any proposition whatever from a contradiction cannot be applied. It follows that a confused metaphysical view can have important practical consequences and may, for example, mean the difference between life and death to a criminal or a heretic.

When, in nineteenth-century England, the rich man brushed aside all consideration for his unsuccessful rivals in the battle for wealth and position, and looking at them as they starved in the gutter said to himself, "Well, they had the same opportunities as I had. If I took more advantage of them than they did, that is not my fault but theirs," he was most probably not only callous but (as I shall try to show) metaphysically confused. A man who said "Heredity and environment made me what I am and made them what they are" would be less likely to fall a prey to this sort of callousness and indifference. Metaphysical views about free will are therefore practically important, and their importance is often in inverse proportion to their clarity.

What is this metaphysical view about free will that I wish to attack? Its supporters usually characterise it negatively, by contrasting it with what it is not, namely determinism on the one hand and pure chance or caprice on the other. This is a dangerous procedure, because a negative characterisation may rule out absolutely every possibility; as if we defined a new sort of natural number, a "free" number, as one which is neither prime nor divisible by a number which is greater than one and smaller than itself. Our negative characterisation, that is, may be so comprehensive as to leave room for no possibility whatever. However let us play the metaphysician's game as long as we can, and let us try to see what the metaphysical doctrine of free will is, at least by investigating what it is not. And what it is not is, first of all, determinism.

"What would become of your laws, your morality, your religion, your gallows, your Paradise, your Gods, your Hell, if it were shown that such and such fluids, such fibres, or a certain acridity in the blood, or in the animal spirits, alone suffice to make a man the object of your punishments or your rewards?" So wrote the notorious

Marquis de Sade.[2] According to Nigel Balchin, "The modern en-
docrinologist sometimes goes far to support de Sade, and draws a
rather humiliating picture of a man as a sort of chemico-electric
experiment, in which a drop too much of this, or a grain too little
of that, is the origin of personality. The psychologist insists that an
apparently minor incident or accident in the early stages of our development may affect the whole course of our lives. In the face of
this comparison of views most of us are inclined to compromise.
We believe that heredity, accident, and incident have a bearing on
man's character and actions, and may even sometimes have a determinative one. But we do not accept the complete suspension of
moral judgment implicit in de Sade's view." [3]

These quotations come from literary, rather than professionally
philosophical sources, but there is nothing in them, I think, which
would not be endorsed by the ablest philosophical defenders of
the metaphysical notion of freedom, for example, C. A. Campbell.
Two comments are important at this stage. The first is that not
only de Sade, but his biographer Nigel Balchin and the philosopher
Campbell, and very many men in the street, hold that to accept
the deterministic position is to give up the notion of moral responsibility. The second is that the view outlined by Balchin does
not entail the absurdity that we can never predict what people will
do. According to Balchin, heredity and environment are important,
though they do not exhaust the matter. And, as Campbell holds,
free will need only be supposed to operate in cases of moral conflict,
when our nature as determined by heredity and environment pulls
us away from the path of duty. Since cases of moral conflict are
rare, we can usually predict people's behaviour just as confidently
as if we believed wholeheartedly in the determinist position. So the
common argument against metaphysical freedom, that it makes
nonsense of our confidence in predicting human behaviour, falls
to the ground. (Hume, for example,[4] pointed out that the condemned prisoner prefers to attack the stone walls of his cell rather
than the inflexible nature of his gaolers.) So I shall not press this
particular objection.

[2] Quoted by Nigel Balchin, *The Anatomy of Villainy*, p. 174.
[3] *Ibid.*, p. 251.
[4] *Treatise* (London: Oxford University Press, 1941), Bk. II, Pt. iii, Sec. 1.

Those who hold that determinism and moral responsibility are incompatible with one another do not, of course, hold that we are responsible for those of our actions which are due to pure chance. Somehow they want our moral choices to be neither determined nor a matter of chance. Campbell has a word for it: he says that our moral choices are instances of "contra-causal freedom." [5] There is not "unbroken causal continuity" in the universe, but we are sometimes able to choose between "genuinely open possibilities." None of these concepts is at all precisely defined by Campbell, but I propose to give definitions of "unbroken causal continuity" and of "pure chance" that may be acceptable to him, and to like-minded thinkers, and I shall then enquire whether in the light of these definitions there is any room for "contra-causal freedom" and "genuinely open possibilities."

(*D1*.) I shall state the view that there is "unbroken causal continuity" in the universe as follows. It is in principle possible to make a sufficiently precise determination of the state of a sufficiently wide region of the universe at time t_0, and sufficient laws of nature are in principle ascertainable to enable a superhuman calculator to be able to predict any event occurring within that region at an already given time t_1.[6]

(*D2*.) I shall define the view that "pure chance" reigns to some extent within the universe as follows. There are some events that even a superhuman calculator could not predict, however precise his knowledge of however wide a region of the universe at some previous time.

These definitions are themselves far from being precise. What does it mean to say that "sufficient laws of nature are in principle ascertainable"? The difficulty here comes from talking of the universe as deterministic or indeterministic. A perfectly precise meaning can be given to saying that certain *theories* are deterministic or indeterministic (for example that Newtonian mechanics is deterministic, quantum mechanics indeterministic), but our talk about actual events in the world as being determined or otherwise may

[5] "Is 'Freewill' a Pseudo-Problem?" *Mind*, LX (1951).
[6] Cf. Laplace: *Théorie Analytique des Probabilités,* second edition (Paris, 1814), p. ii of the Introduction.

be little more than a reflection of our faith in prevailing types of physical theory. It may therefore be that when we apply the adjectives "deterministic" and "indeterministic" to the *universe* as opposed to *theories,* we are using these words in such a way that they have no sense. This consideration does not affect our present inquiry, however. For the believer in free will holds that *no* theory of a deterministic sort or of a pure chance sort will apply to everything in the universe: he must therefore envisage a theory of a type which is neither deterministic nor indeterministic in the senses of these words which I have specified by the two definitions *D1* and *D2;* and I shall argue that no such theory is possible.

In giving a definition of determinism in terms of predictability, moreover, I neglect K. R. Popper's interesting demonstration ("Indeterminism in Quantum Physics and in Classical Physics," *British Journal for the Philosophy of Science,* I, 117–33 and 173–95) that there is a sense in which even within classical physics some events must be unpredictable. If there are two predictors P and Q, they cannot predict one another's behaviour. For by the definition of a predictor, small changes in P must lead to large changes in Q and *vice versa.* So in order for P to predict Q it must predict itself, but it cannot do this, for reasons similar to those in Ryle's *Concept of Mind,* pages 195 and following. In particular, if the Laplacian demon is to predict the universe it cannot itself be part of the universe, nor can it interact with the universe. The notion of a Laplacian demon is thus a physically unrealisable one. However the notion of a Laplacian demon which was nonphysical and which gained information about the world without energy interchanges does seem to be a *logically* possible, though a physically impossible one, and that is enough for present purposes. In any case I do not think that the libertarian would be satisfied by the assertion that human beings have merely that sort of unpredictability in principle that mechanical predictors made of springs, weights, levers and so on might have.

In the sense of *D2* the change of state, at a certain time, of a particular atom of radium would, according to modern quantum theory, be an event of "pure chance." It is important to distinguish "pure chance" from "chance" or "accident." Things may happen by chance or accident in a purely deterministic universe. (More precisely, we can have a use for the words "chance" and "accident" even within a purely deterministic theory.) A man walks along the street and is hit on the head by a falling tile. This is "chance" [7] or "accident" in the sense that it is the result of two separate causal chains, the first involving the causes of his walking along just that route at just that time, the second involving the causes of just that tile falling at just that time. There is no law which explains the event in question, as there would have been if the man had just walked under a ladder and if it had been a law of nature that men who walk under ladders get hit on the head by a falling body within the next thirty seconds. Nevertheless, though the man's being hit on the head is a case of "chance," Laplace's superhuman calculator could have predicted the occurrence. It is not this sense of "chance" that I am meaning when I refer to "pure chance."

Campbell (like Balchin and de Sade) holds that if the whole universe is deterministic in the sense of *D1*, then no one is morally responsible, for on this hypothesis if a person does a certain action "he could not have done otherwise," and that he could have done otherwise is a condition of moral responsibility. Now there is perhaps a sense of "could not have done otherwise" in which whether or not a person could or could not have done otherwise depends on whether or not the universe is deterministic in the sense of *D1*. But it does not follow that if a person could not have done otherwise in this special sense then he could not have done otherwise in any *ordinary* sense. Taken in any ordinary sense, within some concrete context of daily life, "he could have done otherwise" has no metaphysical implications. Does a child have to learn about Laplacian determinism before he can say that his little sister could have eaten her apple instead of his candy? Now it is the ordinary sense which we use when we talk about moral responsibility. How then can it follow that if a person "could not have done otherwise," in the *special* sense, that he was not morally responsible?

Campbell also holds, we may feel sure, that if an action comes about by "pure chance" in the sense of *D2*, then the agent is not morally responsible. He says, for example, that "a man cannot be morally responsible for an act which does not express his own choice

[7] Cf. Aristotle, *Physics*, 196b–97b.

but is, on the contrary, attributable to chance." [8] It is true that a little lower down Campbell uses the word "accident," and by "an accident" we mean "chance" in the weak sense, not "pure chance," but this is obviously a slip of the pen. I am sure that Campbell would agree that if one of our actions happened by "pure chance" in the sense in which, according to modern physics, the change of state of a particular radium atom happens by pure chance, then this action would not be one for which we could be held *responsible*. We may therefore interpret Campbell as holding that if there is such a thing as moral responsibility then people's actions must not always be determined in the sense of *D1*, nor must they happen by pure chance in the sense of *D2:* they must occur as the result of something else, namely "contra-causal freedom."

The difficulty I find in the above conception is as follows. If we accept the definitions *D1* and *D2*, the following propositions are contradictories:

> *p:* This event happened as a result of unbroken causal continuity.
> *q:* This event happened by pure chance.
> That is, *q* if and only if not *p*.
> But *p* or not *p*.
> So *p* or *q*, and not both not *p* and not *q*.

Therefore there is no *third* possibility outside *p* and *q*. What room, then, does logic leave for the concept of "contra-causal freedom?"

Are *D1* and *D2* good definitions of "unbroken causal continuity" and "pure chance"? Campbell might deny that they are, and up to a point I should agree with him. The notions of "causal necessity" and "chance" as used by philosophers are pretty vague, and it is to some extent uncertain just what are the rules of the game when we use these words. I want to show that there are imaginable cases which, if we adhered strictly to *D2*, we should have to call cases of pure chance, but which it would be natural to assimilate to "necessity." But I want also to suggest that any such imaginable cases would only lead us to revise *D1* and *D2* in *this* sense, that what was before "pure chance" would now be-

8 "Is 'Freewill' a Pseudo-Problem?" p. 460.

come "unbroken causal continuity" or *vice versa:* the precise description of an intermediate possibility (a possibility which it would be natural for Campbell to call "contra-causal freedom") must forever elude us. That is, it might be natural to redefine "unbroken causal continuity" and "pure chance" so as to redistribute possible cases between them, but logic leaves me no room for a modification of *D1* and *D2* which would allow me to slap my knee and say "Ah! *That* must be the sort of thing Campbell means by 'contra-causal freedom.'" I shall illustrate my point by means of two examples.

(i) The universe might be such that it would be impossible for Laplace's superhuman calculator to predict a given event *E* from a knowledge of however many laws of nature and a determination, however precise, of however wide a region of the universe, at time t_0. Nevertheless we can conceive that he could calculate the occurrence of *E* from a knowledge of the initial conditions at two different times t_1 and t_2, plus certain laws of nature which would clearly be of a novel type. That is, the laws of nature together with the initial conditions at t_1 would determine not a single possibility but a linear *range* of possibilities, but with a fresh cross-bearing based on conditions at t_2 we should be able to make a unique prediction. In such a universe (or perhaps better, in the case of our having such a picture of the universe) it would be natural to say that *E* was "determined." Nevertheless according to *D1* and *D2* taken as they stand it would be a matter of "pure chance." We might make an appropriate modification of *D1* and *D2* so that this was no longer so.

(ii) The universe might consist of two regions *A* and *B* such that from a complete knowledge of the state of *A* at time t_1 together with a complete knowledge of the state of *B* at time t_2 you could predict the occurrence of any event *E* occurring in *A* at t_2, though from the state of the whole universe at t_1 no such prediction could be made. According to *D1* and *D2*, taken strictly, *E* would have to be said to occur by "pure chance," but it might be natural, if such a universe (or such a type of law of nature) were more than a theoretical possibility, to remodel *D1* and *D2* so that *E* would now be said to occur "by necessity." For I do not think that a philosopher like Campbell would be inclined to call a moral choice "free" if it could be predicted from a knowledge of a previous state of a part of the universe in which the event took place together with a knowledge of the present state of a different part of the universe.

The above two examples show how there might be formulated a novel type of natural law which would be quasi-deterministic— that is, which would not be deterministic in the strict sense of *D1* but which nevertheless would be such that we should feel like modifying *D1* to accommodate it. (Of course if we did find it useful to formulate laws of such types we should find ourselves involved in a radical revolution in physical theory: the new physics would probably be at least as far removed from present-day physics as quantum theory is from classical physics.) But could any such case of quasi-determinism be accepted as a case of "contra-causal freedom?" Thinking of these cases may induce us to modify *D1* and *D2* so that the frontier between "necessity" and "pure chance" is moved a little one way or another, but this will not provide us with a buffer zone between the two territories.

Campbell holds that if determinism in the sense of *D1* is true then a man could never correctly be said to have been able to do otherwise than he did. That this is not so can be seen if we consider the following example. Suppose that when washing the dishes you drop a plate, but that fortunately it does not break. You say, however, that it *could* have broken. That is, within the range of possible initial conditions covered by possible cases of "dropping," the known dispositional characteristics of the plate do not allow us to rule out the proposition "it will break." If, however, it had been an aluminium plate, then it would not have broken. That is, whatever the initial conditions had been (within a wide range) it would not have broken. Whether dropped flat or on its edge, with a spinning motion or with no spinning motion, from three feet or four feet or five feet, it still would not have broken. Thus such cases in which we use the words "could have" or "could not have" are cases in which we either cannot or can use a law or a law-like proposition to rule out a certain possibility despite our uncertainty as to the precise initial conditions. Briefly: E could not have happened if there are laws or law-like propositions which rule out E. Campbell wants to use "could not have happened" in a different way: he will say that E could not have happened if E is ruled out by certain laws or law-like propositions *together with the initial conditions.*[9]

However it is pretty certain that Campbell would resist the suggestion that "John Smith could have done otherwise" is analogous to "the plate could have broken." He would say[10] that it is an actual particular person in a particular set of circumstances with whom we are concerned when we ask "Could he have done otherwise? Was he morally responsible?" and that we are in no way concerned with hypothetical possibilities. It is difficult to see the force of this sort of criticism. It is but a tautology to say that if we ask whether John Smith could have done otherwise then we are asking a question about John Smith. Clearly we are interested in John Smith as an individual who has to deal with a particular situation, but what follows? That nothing follows can be made evident if we develop our example of the dropped plate. Suppose that I have a very valuable plate, made in China and once the property of some ancient emperor and the only one of its kind. While showing it to a friend I drop it but fortunately it does not break. Gasping with relief I say, "It could have broken but thank goodness it did not." Here we are using the words "could have" and yet our interest is very much in this particular plate in this set of circumstances. There is no suggestion here, however, that a very precise determination of the initial conditions together with an exact knowledge of the physical properties of the plate would not have enabled us to predict that in these (rather fortunate) circumstances it would not break.

On this analysis "could have" implies "would have if certain conditions had been fulfilled." In moral contexts the conditions that are of most importance are "if he had chosen," "if he had tried," and "if he had wanted to." This is not to say that in some

[9] For a discussion of this sort of point see F. V. Raab, "Free Will and the Ambiguity of 'Could,'" *Philosophical Review*, LXIV (1955), 60–77.
[10] "Is 'Freewill' a Pseudo-Problem?" p. 453.

cases we may not mean more than this. J. L. Austin, in a British Academy lecture,[11] has recently argued that whether or no determinism be the case, it is certainly contrary to what is suggested by ordinary language and ordinary thought. For example in part of an interesting footnote he says:[12]

"Consider the case where I miss a very short putt and kick myself because I could have holed it. It is not that I should have holed it if I had tried: I did try and missed. It is not that I should have holed it if conditions had been different: that might of course be so, but I am talking about conditions as they precisely were, and asserting that I could have holed it. There's the rub."

To elucidate this passage compare the sentence "I could have holed it if I had tried" with the sentence "this plate could have broken if it had been colder weather." This does not mean that it *would* have broken if had been colder weather. For a metal plate that becomes brittle due to intense cold may nevertheless be lucky in the way it falls, like the china plate in my example. When I say that I could have holed the putt (though I tried to and failed) I mean that I could have even if the *external* conditions had been precisely the same. It is surely compatible with this ordinary way of talking that I believe, like any determinist, that if the external conditions *and* the internal conditions (the state of my brain and nervous system) were precisely reproduced then my failure to hole the putt would be precisely reproduced. I cannot see, therefore, that Austin has shown that ordinary language favours indeterminism. Not that this matter is very important philosophically. Ordinary language may well enshrine a falsehood. Austin himself clearly distinguishes between the question of whether determinism is the case and the question of whether it is implied in ordinary language. Certainly Austin's careful discussion of "can" does not help me to guess what Campbell might mean by the word, for I can deal with all of Austin's cases on the lines of my china plate example. This is not to deny the intrinsic interest in many of Austin's suggestions, such as that the "if" in "I can if I choose" is not the conditional "if" familiar to logicians but is the "if" of doubt or

[11] "Ifs and Cans," *Proceedings of the British Academy* (1956), pp. 109–32.
[12] *Ibid.*, p. 119.

hesitation. (Compare: "I can, but do I choose?" "I can but whether I choose to do so or not is another question." [13])

We can now consider Campbell's phrase "genuinely open possibility." If I drop a china plate it is an open possibility that it will break. It is not an open possibility that an aluminium plate will break. The possibility of an aluminium plate breaking can be ruled out for any likely range of initial conditions from a knowledge of the physical properties of aluminium. Whether the aluminium plate is dropped on its side or on its edge, with a rotary motion or without a rotary motion, in hot weather or cold weather, from a height of two feet or six feet, it still will not break. With the china plate, in some of these cases it will break and in some not. The phrases "an open possibility" and "not an open possibility" are therefore easily understood. What about "genuinely open possibility?" We might suggest that a possibility is "genuinely open" if from the relevant laws and law-like propositions together with a determination, however precise, of the initial conditions, not even Laplace's superhuman calculator could predict what will happen. This is, by *D2*, just a case of pure chance. Once more our endeavour to describe something intermediate between determinism and pure chance has failed.

Campbell tries by introspection to distinguish "contra-causal freedom" from both "causal necessitation" and "pure chance." That is, he hopes by appealing to introspection to give a sense to "could have done otherwise" which is different from both that in (*a*) "the plate could have broken" and that in (*b*) "even if the initial conditions had been precisely the same that atom could have shot out a photon." His appeal to introspection is an appeal to our feeling that in certain situations we can do either of two alternative things. Well, in certain situations I certainly do feel that I can do either of two things. That is, I say to myself, "I can do this and I can do that." *Either* I say this to myself using "can" in an ordinary way (as in "the plate could break, and it could fall without breaking") *or* I say these words to myself using "can" in some new way. In the former case introspection has yielded no

---

[13] These and other examples of this sort of "if" are given by Austin, "Ifs and Cans," pp. 114–15.

new sense of "can," and in the latter case some new use of "can" must already have been established. For unless this new use of "can" can be explained antecedently to such introspection, introspection will only yield the fact of my saying to myself a meaningless sentence. But, as I have already argued, logic leaves no room for such a new sense of "can."

A similar situation arises if any alternative description of the predicament of moral choice is attempted. Thus Campbell says[14] that "I further find, if I ask myself just what it is I am believing when I believe that I 'can' rise to duty, that I cannot help believing that it lies with me here and now quite absolutely, which of two genuinely open possibilities I adopt." Our reply must be that we cannot say whether this is so or not. Perhaps we believe this, perhaps we do not, but we cannot tell until Campbell can explain to us what he means by "lies with me here and now quite absolutely" (as opposed to "lies with me here and now"), and until he can explain what is meant by "genuinely open possibilities" (as opposed to "open possibilities"). The same difficulty crops up[15] when he appeals to "creative activity." "Granted that creative activity is possible . . . ," he says. But in any ordinary sense of these words creative activity is not only possible but actual. There are poets, novelists, mathematicians, architects and inventors. In what sense of "creative activity" is it an open question whether creative activity is possible or not? Some writers again bring in the concept of "spontaneity." But you do not have to reject metaphysical determinism before you can believe that your rubbish heap burst into flames as a result of spontaneous combustion.

Most of our ordinary senses of "could have" and "could not have" are not, in my view, incompatible with determinism. Though some of our ordinary talk about moral responsibility is frequently vitiated by a confused metaphysics of free will, much of it can be salvaged.

When in a moral context we say that a man could have or could not have done something we are concerned with the ascription of responsibility. What is it to ascribe responsibility? Suppose Tommy

---

[14] "Is 'Freewill' a Pseudo-Problem?" p. 463.
[15] *Ibid.*, p. 462.

at school does not do his homework. If the schoolmaster thinks that this is because Tommy is really very stupid, then it is silly of him to abuse Tommy, to cane him or to threaten him. This would be sensible only if it were the case that this sort of treatment made stupid boys intelligent. With the possible exception of certain nineteenth-century schoolmasters, no one has believed this. The schoolmaster says, then, that Tommy is not to blame, he just *could not* have done his homework. Now suppose that the reason why Tommy did not do his homework is that he was lazy: perhaps he had just settled down to do it when some other boy tempted him to come out and climb a tree. In such a case the schoolmaster will hold Tommy responsible, and he will say that Tommy could have done his homework. By this he will not necessarily mean to deny that Tommy's behaviour was the outcome of heredity and environment. The case is similar to that of the plate which could have broken. The lazy boy is analogous to the china plate which could break and also could fall without breaking. The stupid boy is like the aluminium plate: whatever the initial conditions the same thing happens. If Tommy is sufficiently stupid, then it does not matter whether he is exposed to temptation or not exposed to temptation, threatened or not threatened, cajoled or not cajoled. When his negligence is found out, he is not made less likely to repeat it by threats, promises, or punishments. On the other hand, the lazy boy can be influenced in such ways. Whether he does his homework or not is perhaps solely the outcome of environment, but one part of the environment is the threatening schoolmaster.

Threats and promises, punishments and rewards, the ascription of responsibility and the nonascription of responsibility, have therefore a clear pragmatic justification which is quite consistent with a wholehearted belief in metaphysical determinism. Indeed it implies a belief that our actions are very largely determined: if everything anyone did depended only on pure chance (*i.e.* if it depended on nothing) then threats and punishments would be quite ineffective. But even a libertarian of course may admit that *most* of our actions are pretty well determined. (Campbell excepts only those acts which are done from a sense of duty against our inclination.)

It begins to appear that the metaphysical question of determinism is quite irrelevant to the rationality of our ascription of responsibility.

What about praise and blame? These concepts are more difficult. We must at the outset distinguish two ways in which we commonly use the word "praise." In one sense praise is the opposite of blame. We praise Tommy for his industry, blame him for his laziness. But when we praise a girl for her good looks this does not mean that we should have blamed her if her looks had been bad. When we praise one footballer for his brilliant run, we do not blame his unfortunate teammate who fumbled a pass. (Unless, of course, the fumble was due to carelessness.) When we praise Smith for his mathematical talent we do not imply that we blame Jones because, try as hard as he may, he cannot handle x's and y's. Of course we may well say that a girl is ugly, a footballer incompetent, or a man unmathematical, and this is the opposite of praise. But it is not blame. Praise and dispraise, in this sense, is simply grading a person as good or bad in some way. A young philosopher may feel pleasure at being praised by one of his eminent colleagues because he thereby knows that his work is assessed highly by one who is competent to judge, and he may be pained to hear himself dispraised because he thereby knows that his work is being assessed as of poor quality. Praise and dispraise of this sort has an obvious function just as has the grading of apples.[16] A highly graded apple is bought and a highly graded philosopher is appointed to a lectureship, while a low graded apple is not bought and the low graded philosopher is not appointed.

In general to praise or dispraise a man, a woman's nose, or a footballer's style is to grade it, and if the grader is competent we feel sure that there are good reasons for the grading. In practice, of course, reasons are frequently given, and this giving of reasons in itself can constitute what is called praise or dispraise. For example, if a philosopher writes about some candidate for a lectureship that he has some illuminating new ideas about the logic of certain psychological concepts, this is the sort of thing that is

[16] On the notion of grading, see J. O. Urmson's article "On Grading," in A. G. N. Flew, ed., *Logic and Language* (Oxford: Blackwell, 1955), Second Series, pp. 159–88.

meant by "praise," and if he says that the candidate is muddle-headed and incapable of writing clear prose, this is the sort of thing which is meant by "dispraise." It is not the sort of thing we mean when we contrast praise with blame. To say that a man cannot write clear prose is not necessarily to blame him. He may have been brought up among muddle-headed people and always given muddle-headed books to read. The fact that we do not feel like blaming him, however, does not alter the fact that we warn prospective employers about him.

Just as we may praise or dispraise a woman for her figure, a footballer for his fleetness or slowness of foot, a lecturer in philosophy for his intelligence or lack of intelligence, and a writer for clarity or obscurity, so naturally enough, we may praise or dispraise a man for his honesty or dishonesty, truthfulness or untruthfulness, kindness or unkindness and so on. In *this* sense of "praise" we may praise moral qualities and moral actions in exactly the same way as we may praise beauty, intelligence, agility, or strength. Either we may do so quite generally, using a grading word like "good," "excellent," or "first-class," or we may simply give a description. (For example: her cheeks are like roses, her eyes are like stars.) Praise has a primary function and a secondary function. In its primary function it is just to tell people what people are like. To say that one candidate for a lectureship writes clear prose whereas another cannot put a decent sentence together is to help the committee to decide who should be given the lectureship. Naturally enough, therefore, we like to be praised, hate to be dispraised. And even if no actual advantage is to come from praise, we like to be praised by a competent judge for work we have done because we take this as evidence that we have been on the right track and done something valuable. Because we come to like being praised and to hate being dispraised, praise and dispraise come to have an important secondary function. To praise a class of actions is to encourage people to do actions of that class. And utility of an action normally, but not always, corresponds to utility of praise of it.

So far I have talked of praise and dispraise, not of praise and blame. This is because I wanted a contrary for "praise" in the sense in which we can praise not only a moral action but a woman's nose. What about the contrast of praise with blame? Here I suggest that a clear-headed man will use the word "praise" just as before, and the word "blame" just like the previous "dispraise," with one proviso. This is that to praise (in this sense) or to blame a person for an action is not only to grade it (morally) but to imply that it is something for which the person is responsible, in the perfectly ordinary and nonmetaphysical sense of "responsible" which we have analysed earlier in this article. So we blame Tommy for his bad homework if this is due to laziness, not if it is due to stupidity. Blame in this sense can be just as dispassionate as dispraise of a woman's nose: it is just a grading plus an ascription of responsibility. It is perfectly compatible with a recognition that the lazy Tommy is what he is simply as a result of heredity plus environment (and perhaps pure chance).

Now most men do not, in my opinion, praise and blame people in this dispassionate and clear-headed way. This is brought out, in fact, by the quotations from de Sade and Balchin: most men do *not* feel that blame, in the way they use the word "blame," would be appropriate if a man's action was the result of heredity plus environment. The appropriateness of praise and blame is bound up, in the eyes of the ordinary man, with a notion of freewill which is quite metaphysical. Admittedly this metaphysics is incoherent and unformulated (as indeed it has to be, for when formulated it becomes self-contradictory). Nevertheless we can see that a rather pharisaical attitude to sinners and an almost equally unhealthy attitude to saints is bound up with this metaphysics in the thinking of the ordinary man if we look at the way in which very often his whole outlook and tendency to *judge* (not just to grade) other men changes when he is introduced to, and becomes convinced by, a philosophical analysis of freewill like the one in the present paper. How, again, can we explain the idea, held by so many religious people, that an omnipotent and benevolent God can *justly* condemn people to an eternity of torture? Must we not suppose that they have some confused idea that even with the same heredity and environmental influences, and quite apart from pure chance, the sinner *could* have done otherwise? (Of course, even granting this, the utility of Hell in the eyes of a benevolent God still remains obscure.) Or consider the man who excuses himself for his indifference to his less fortunate neighbour by saying, "Hadn't he the same opportunities as I had? He could have got on if he had acted with my drive, initiative, and so forth." There is sense in such a remark only in so far as the contempt for laziness and lack of drive to which it gives expression is socially useful in spurring others on to display more drive than they otherwise would.

But a man's drive is determined by his genes and his environment, and such a remark as the one above is after all a rather unimportant part of the environment. So I do not think that the remark can be regarded as just a way of influencing people to display drive and resourcefulness. It does depend on a metaphysics of free will. After all, if everyone had the genes that make for drive and energy they could not *all* get to the top. Dog would still eat dog.

The upshot of the discussion is that we should be quite as ready to *grade* a person for his moral qualities as for his nonmoral qualities, but we should stop *judging* him. (Unless "judge" just means "grade," as in "judging apples.") Moreover, if blame in general is irrational, so must be self-blame or self-reproach, unless this comes simply to resolving to do better next time.

Bibliographical Essay

~~~~~~

The student who wishes to pursue further the issues discussed in this volume will find the following works useful. No attempt is made at being comprehensive.

Anthologies: BERNARD BEROFSKY's *Free Will and Determinism* (New York: Harper & Row, Publishers, 1966); KEITH LEHRER's *Freedom and Determinism* (New York: Random House, Inc., 1966); H. MORRIS' *Freedom and Responsibility* (Stanford, Calif.: Stanford University Press, 1966); MORGANBESSER and WALSH, *Free Will* (Englewood Cliffs, N.J.: Prentice-Hall, Inc., 1962); SIDNEY HOOK's *Determinism and Freedom in the Age of Modern Science* (New York: Collier, 1961); and D. F. PEARS's *Freedom and the Will* (London: Macmillan & Co. Ltd., 1963). In addition, PAP and ED-WARD's *A Modern Introduction to Philosophy* (New York: Free Press, 1965) contains an excellent and extensive selected bibliography on this topic. The Morris book is particularly valuable for articles dealing with related issues such as responsibility and punishment.

For other historically influential examples of the "soft" determinist position (the compatability of determinism and free will) besides Hume: J. S. MILL's *An Examination of Sir William Hamilton's Philosophy* (London: Longmans, Green & Co. Ltd., 1872); A. J. AYER's "Freedom and Necessity," reprinted in his *Philosophical Essays* (London: Macmillan & Co. Ltd., 1954); R. B HOBART's "Free Will as Involving Indetermination and Inconceivable Without It," *Mind,* XLIII 1934. For "hard" determinism: BARON HOLBACH's

System of Nature, excerpts from which are printed in Pap and Edwards. An interesting defense of indeterminism may be found in HENRI BERGSON's *Time and Free Will* (London: Macmillan & Co. Ltd., 1921). C. A. Campbell has insisted upon the irreconcilability of determinism and free will and the truth of the latter in a number of works, most recently in *Of Selfhood and Godhood* (London: Macmillan, 1957). There are a number of articles on the relationship of predictability to free will, including: D. M. McKAYS' "On the Logical Indeterminacy of a Free Choice," *Mind*, LXIX 1960; J. CANFIELD's "Determinism, Free Will and the Ace Predictor," *Mind*, LXX 1961; ALVIN GOLDMAN's "Actions, Predictions and Books Of Life," *American Philosophical Quarterly*, V 1968; HAMPSHIRE AND HART's "Decision, Intention and Certainty," *Mind*, LXVII 1958; and K. LEHRER's "Decisions and Causes," *Philosophical Review*, LXXII 1963.

There is an extensive literature on the analysis of "can" statements. The Moore position presented in this volume is attacked by John Austin in "Ifs and Cans," reprinted in his *Philosophical Papers* (Oxford: 1961). Other discussions include: R. TAYLOR, "I Can," *Philosophical Review*, LXIX 1960; F. V. RAAB, "Free Will and the Ambiguity of 'Could,'" *Philosophical Review*, LXIV 1955; R. D. BRADLEY, " 'Ifs,' 'Cans' and Determinism," *Australasian Journal of Philosophy*, XL 1962; and A. M. HONORE, "Can and Can't," *Mind*, LXXIII 1964.

Much contemporary discussion goes on in terms of what some philosophers call Action Theory, dealing with such questions as: What is a reason, and how does it differ from a cause? Can we give causal explanations of human actions? What is the difference between a voluntary and an involuntary act? A useful collection of articles, as well as a bibliography, may be found in A. WHITE's *The Philosophy of Action* (Oxford: Oxford University Press 1968). A difficult but rewarding article by D. PEARS, "Desires as Causes of Action," appears in *Royal Institute of Philosophy Lectures*, Vol. I (London: Macmillan & Co. Ltd., 1968).

The implications of determinism for our currently accepted attitudes and practices towards people—for example, praise, blame, and punishment—may be found in J. D. MABBOTT, "Free Will and Punishment"; in H. D. LEWIS, *Contemporary British Philosophy*,

Third Series (London: George Allen and Unwin Ltd., 1956); H. L. A. HART, "Legal Responsibility and Excuses," in Hook, *op. cit.;* W. I. MATSON, "On the Irrelevance of Free Will to Moral Responsibility and the Vacuity of the Later," *Mind,* LXV 1956; E. L. BEARDSLEY, "Determinism and Moral Perspectives," *Philosophy and Phenomenological Research,* XX, 1960; P. H. NOWELL-SMITH, "Freewill and Moral Responsibility," *Mind,* LVII 1948; BLUMENFELD and DWORKIN, "Necessity, Contingency and Punishment," *Philosophical Studies,* XVI 1965; H. KELSEN, "Causality and Retribution," in *What Is Justice* (Los Angeles: University of California Press, 1957).